KIDS DISCOVER

DENVER AND BOULDER

A Guide to Family Fun and Adventure

Delightful Descriptions
by Sara Goodman Zimet

Cover Illustration
by Sandy Ferguson Fuller

**Published by
Discovery Press Publications**

First Edition Copyright ©1995 Discovery Press Publications, Sara Goodman Zimet
PO Box 201502, Denver CO 80220-7502 USA
Cover illustration Copyright ©1995 Sandy Ferguson Fuller, Alp Arts Co.

ISBN 0-9645159-0-3

Printed in the United States of America
10 9 8 7 6 5 4 3 2 1

**For Patrick and Hannah,
My Inspirations**

ACKNOWLEDGEMENTS

There are many people who played a variety of roles which led to the completion of this book and who are deserving of my deepest appreciation. First, there are two who are responsible for setting the project in motion, my grandchildren, Patrick and Hannah Zimet. If I hadn't been inspired to entice them to Denver for longer and longer visits, this guidebook never would have seen the light of day.

Then, of course, there were those who stood along the sidelines, cheered me on, and made some very helpful suggestions. Many thanks to Lynne Sturm and Gregory Zimet, Flo Chrusciel and Andy Zimet, Sue Lubeck, Elsa Folsom, Rosalie and Don Schiff, Janet Mackenzie, Ruth Loewi, Lily Appelman, Jo and Dick Sanders, Chris and Herschel Berkowitz, and especially to my husband, Carl Zimet.

For excellent professional guidance and technical assistance, I am indebted to Sandy Ferguson Fuller, Matt Harding, and Freddie Snalam.

I spoke to many people in the various places described in this guidebook, both in person and over the telephone. My gratitude extends to Gail Bell, Debbie Long, Patti Quitugua, Rene Munoz, and Moya Suddaby-Bennett. Unfortunately, most of my contacts were anonymous contributors who graciously answered my many questions and sent me images for use in this guide without attaching their names. If they should come across Kids Discover Denver and Boulder and recall talking with me, I want them to know that I am grateful for the time they took to inform me.

When it came time to ask for images from some of the places described in the guide book, the following people responded quickly and graciously to my requests: Gail Bell, Angela Baier, Coral Bright, Laura Douglas, Diane Fatheree, Richard Fuller, Becky Lindz, Debbie Long, Rita Lovato, Patti Quitugua, Anita Razo, Geraldine Stepp, Moya Suddaby-Bennett, Amy Takansik, and Ann Watson.

Finally, I owe a special debt of thanks to Denver and Boulder and its surrounding towns, for providing me with the wealth of fabulous places for children and their families to explore and discover together. My horizons were broadened by the experience of preparing this guide. I hope that all of its readers will enjoy the same sense of pleasure in discovery as I did.

Table of Contents

Chapter 3.
Watching Wildlife: Animals of Colorado and from around the World 65

Chapter 4.
Exploring Worlds: Indoor and Outdoor Museums 85

My turn to drive!
Photo: Zimet-family Archives

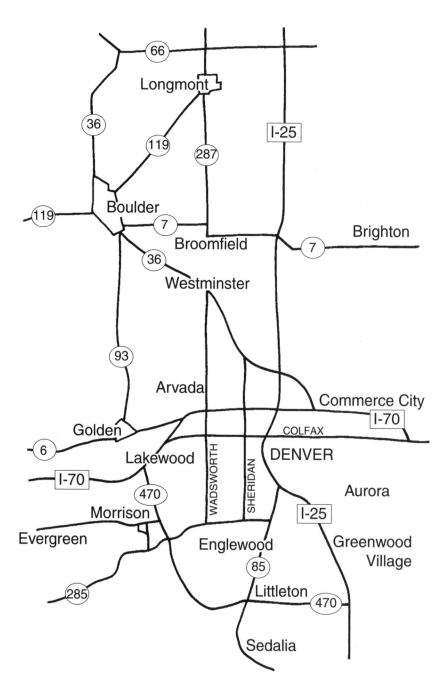

Towns and Cities included in this Guide

CHAPTER 1

Welcome to: Kids Discover Denver and Boulder

How to use this guide

Kids Discover Denver and Boulder was designed to be child- and adult-friendly. As you will read below, this guide was planned to make the identification of interesting places to visit finger-tip easy by using the Table of Contents, the Town Index, or the General Index.

Of paramount concern in selecting a place to visit is to capture your child's interest. The first paragraph of each place description in Kids Discover Denver and Boulder, has attempted to do this. If the approach I took doesn't ring true for your child, use your own words in their place.

In this guide, each chapter focuses on a different theme. If your child is very active and enjoys physical activity, Chapter 2, *Keeping Fit: Playgrounds, Entertainment Centers, and Amusement Parks* will provide many resources for you. Perhaps at another time, you would want to combine physical activity with the opportunity to learn something about animals, alive or extinct, or about Colorado's history. Chapter 3, *Watching Wildlife: Animals in Colorado and from Around the World*, and Chapter 4, *Exploring Worlds: Indoor and Outdoor Museums*, will be your best resources.

If you'd like to introduce your child to the larger world of the arts and spectator sports, you can find it in theaters, concert halls, bookstores, libraries, and stadiums. Chapter 5, *Having More Fun: Plays, Films, Dance, Music, Stories, and Ball Games*, will point you in the right direction.

Then again, you may want to make a special outing to a fair or festival, particularly at holiday times. Browse through

Chapter 6, *Looking Ahead: Adventures by the Month*. It lists special events that recur each year, starting in January and continuing through December.

Another area of importance for any guidebook, is for you to be as informed as possible about what to expect at the place you choose to visit. Providing you with the basic facts is accomplished in outline form in the second part of each place description. You'll find out where the place is and how to drive there. Phone numbers are given and you're told about parking availability and public transportation that stops nearby. The dates, days, and hours it is open, it's admission fees, and information about it's exhibits or presentations are detailed. You also are told if it is accessible by wheelchair, and if food and restrooms are available. If a place hosts birthday parties, this information is also included. Chapter 6 is the exception to this format. Instead, the basic details include a description of the event, the place where the event is held, and the phone number to call for dates, times, and fees.

Standard rates for admission are given if this information is available. However, discounts may be obtainable through group rates, frequent-user cards, American Automobile Association membership, discount coupon books, and various other promotions. Keep this in mind when reading the newspapers and checking through your mail. And don't be bashful about asking before buying your ticket. Many of the places listed are free to all or to some. Free parking and admission are highlighted throughout Kids Discover Denver and Boulder.

Some of the facts may have changed since the printing of Kids Discover Denver and Boulder. It's a good idea, therefore, to call before going to a place, and avoid surprise or disappointment.

Kids Discover Denver and Boulder includes a third set of information when it fits...a list of related places of interest. For example, if your child should be consumed by a preoccupation with cars, dolls, or dinosaurs, you might find it useful to know of other places than the one you are visiting, where this interest can be deepened. If there are none, this part of the place description was excluded.

Getting Where You're Going Without A Car

The map on the page prior to Chapter 1, shows the towns and cities where the places described in Kids Discover Denver and Boulder are to be found. An underlying assumption of this guide is that you will be driving to these places. Where driving directions are given, they originate in downtown Denver for Denver metropolitan area places, and in downtown Boulder for Boulder places. If you are coming from another part of the metropolitan area, call the place you plan to visit and ask for directions from that location.

For those who prefer other modes of transportation, the following information on alterative ways of getting where you're going should be helpful.

Take the bus (Denver:299-6000; Boulder:443-0100). The Denver Regional Transportation District (RTD) buses have their busiest hours from 6:00 to 9:00 a.m. and from 4:00 to 6:00 p.m., Mondays through Fridays. It costs more to travel during those hours, $1.00 for everyone. At all other times, the fare is 50 cents for most people; only 15 cents for those 65 and older, with identification; and 25 cents for disabled people, with identification. Be sure to bring the exact change for your fare. In the summer, June through August, RTD offers a "Just for Youth Bus Pass," for those 18 years old and under, at $7.00 a month. All buses have wheelchair lifts.

The Boulder RTD buses charge one fare for all during peak hours, 60 cents, 6:00 to 9:00 a.m. and 4:00 to 6:00 p.m. However, during off-peak hours, senior adults pay 15 cents and disabled persons, 25 cents. Remember to bring the exact change.

Take the Light Rail Transit (Denver: 299-6000). The Light Rail Transit (LRT), also known as the Metro Area Connection (MAC), runs in Denver from South Broadway, near the Gates Rubber Plant, to 30th Street and Welton Avenue, with several stops in between, including the Auraria College Campus. The fare structure is the same as for RTD buses, and transfers are valid between RTD and LRT. Passengers must buy tickets from the machines located at each stop which make change. They will not accept tokens, pennies, or any bills above $20. Fares vary, depending on the time of day you travel. All trains have wheelchair lifts.

Take the Sixteenth Street Mall Shuttle (Denver: 299-6000). The Shuttle runs along the Sixteenth Street Mall in downtown Denver between Broadway and Market Street and is free to all users.

Take the Cultural Connection Trolley (Denver: 299-6000). The Cultural Connection Trolley is really a bus which is decorated to look like a trolley. It runs from 9:30 a.m. to 5:50 p.m., Mondays through Sundays, from early May through the middle of October. The fare is $2.00 a day for everyone, except children under five years old ride free. Tickets may be purchased from the "trolley" driver or from other places that sell them. Call for this information. It is wheelchair-lift equipped.

The "trolley" runs every 30 minutes and stops at over 20 places that are listed in this guide. I let you know which stops these are in my descriptions under Other

Transportation. You can stop at any place and reboard at any time that same day. Call 299-6000 for more information about where to buy tickets in advance and which stop is closest to you.

Take the Platte Valley Trolley (Denver: 458-6255). The Platte Valley Trolley is a real, open-air trolley. It runs every day, 11:00 a.m. to 4:00 p.m., from June 1st to early September in Denver. The rest of the year, it runs on good-weather weekends only, from 11:00 a.m. to 3:00 p.m. The trips last a half-hour except for one-hour excursions to 12th Street and Sheridan Boulevard, Mondays through Fridays at 12 noon, and Saturdays and Sundays at 2:00 p.m. The fare on the half-hour tour for children and senior adults is $1.00 and for all others is $2.00. For the one hour excursion, the fare for children is $2.00, for senior adults, $3.00, and for all others, $4.00. Wheelchair access is at the Children's Museum only. RTD buses stop nearby.

The Trolley travels on a rail that runs along the Platte River, starting at Confluence Park and 15th Street. The Forney Transportation Museum is located here as well. After you visit the Transportation Museum, you can hop on over to the Children's Museum. You could continue on to see a game at McNichols Sports Arena or at Mile High Stadium, and stop at the Museum on the way back to your car or to the RTD bus that brought you there. By the way, during the game seasons, trolley-runs are scheduled to coincide with the start and finish of the games.

Take a Hop (Boulder: 447-8282). The eight HOP buses shuttle passengers to the three main activity centers in Boulder and points in between. The HOP connects Downtown, the University of Colorado, and the Crossroad Shopping Mall, Mondays to Fridays, from 7:00 a.m. to 7:00 p.m. Shuttles circulate in both directions on a continuous loop, stopping at each shuttle stop every ten minutes. Senior adults pay 15 cents; all others, 25 cents; RTD bus passes and transfers are accepted for free rides. The buses are brightly colored with graphics of rabbits, crickets, and frogs...easily recognized.

Join the *Kids Discover Denver and Boulder Club*

You are invited to become a member of the *Kids Discover Denver and Boulder Club*. If you decide to join, you will receive the following benefits:

1. A membership badge with *Kids Discover Denver and Boulder Club* printed on it.

2. Your name will be included as a contributor to the revised edition of the guidebook, Kids Discover Denver and Boulder.

In order to become a member, you will need to send me the following information:

1. The names of your five most favorite and your five least favorite places from those that are listed in Kids Discover Denver and Boulder.

2. The names and addresses of any places that are not listed but which you think should be.

3. Your name and address so that your name will be included as a contributor to the revised edition of Kids Discover Denver and Boulder and so that you can be sent a membership badge with *Kids Discover Denver and Boulder Club* printed on it.

Send the above information to:

Kids Discover Denver and Boulder Club
Discovery Press Publications
P.O. Box 201502 - A
Denver, Colorado 80220-7502

Author's Disclaimer
In spite of my best efforts, there may be mistakes in the information provided and some typographical errors may have crept into the text. I apologize for these mishaps. No one place is recommended over any other. I leave those judgments to the children and families using this guide and hope that they will become members of the *Kids Discover Denver and Boulder Club* and inform me of their preferences.

Just hanging out!

Photo: Zimet-family Archives

CHAPTER 2

Keeping Fit: Playgrounds, Entertainment Centers and Amusement Parks

Most of us like to have fun and to be physically fit. I discovered that you can do both at the same time. There are many wonderful places, indoors and outdoors, where you can run and roll, climb and crawl, jump and bounce, swing and slide, ski and skate, swim and sail, hike and bike, and do just about anything else you can think of...and even some things you probably had never thought of doing! This chapter tells you where these places are and all the vigorous things you can do when you get there.

Southshore Water Park.

Photo: Southshore Water Park

INDOOR PLAYGROUNDS AND ENTERTAINMENT CENTERS

DISCOVERY ZONE FUN CENTERS
AND LEAPS AND BOUNDS

Do you want to walk on the moon, jump on a water bed, crawl through tunnels, swim in huge ball-bins, travel on a roller slide, meander through a maze, and twist through an obstacle course? Discovery Zone Fun Centers and Leaps and Bounds are the places for you. Each has it's own special activities and they're all fun, fun, fun!

Where are they? Discovery Zone recently bought Leaps and Bounds at the following four locations: 8100 West Crestline Avenue, between Bowles and Belleview in Littleton, in the Cub Food shopping center; 7510 Parkway Drive, at County Line Road and Quebec Street in Littleton; 8230 West 80th Avenue and Carr Street in Arvada, in the Cooper 6 Movies center; and one due to open in Aurora. A Discovery Zone is due to open in 1995 in Westminster at 88th Street and Wadsworth Boulevard. I was informed that, eventually, they will all come under the Discovery Zone name.

Phone numbers? Littleton at Bowles, 979-7938; Littleton at County Line Road, 649-1831; Arvada, 431-9480; Westminster, unknown at the time of printing this guide.

Parking? Yes, and it's free.

Other transportation? RTD buses stop nearby.

Open What days and hours? Mondays through Thursdays, 9:00 a.m. to 9:00 p.m.; Fridays and Saturdays, 9:00 a.m. to 10:00 p.m.; Sundays 11:00 a.m. to 7:00 p.m.

Admission fees? Children 18 months to 12 years old, $5.99; children under 18 months and adults, free. Additional games are available but cost extra.

Supervision? Discovery Zone: Zone Coaches help supervise and initiate games. There are two "sitter" programs available. One is called Break-Time and costs $8.99 for a two-hour period for one child and $7.99 for each additional child; a third hour costs $2.00. The other program is only offered on Tuesdays, Wednesdays, and Thursdays and costs $5.99 plus a special card from the Aurora Mall. Leaps and Bounds: Parents are expected to stay with their children.

Wheelchair accessible? Yes.
Food? Yes.
Restrooms? Yes.
Birthday parties? Yes.

FANTASTIC FUN

Here's what Fantastic Fun has for you: rides on a train, a horse carousel, a ferris wheel, and a swing; a climb on a huge spider web; a swim in a large ball room; and a visit to a giant air castle. And, if you happen to be between 18 months and 3 years old, there's Tiny Tyke Village. It was planned just for you.

Where is it? At 3085 South Broadway in Denver.
Phone number? 761-8701.
Parking? Yes, and it's <u>free</u>.
Other transportation? RTD buses stop nearby.
Open what days and hours? Mondays through Saturdays, 10:00 a.m. to 9:00 p.m.; Sundays, 11:00 a.m. to 6:00 p.m.
Admission fees? Children, $5.95 Thursdays to Mondays and $2.95 Tuesdays and Wednesdays; adults, free.

Supervision? Parents are expected to stay with their children.
Wheelchair accessible? Yes.
Food? Yes.
Restrooms? Yes.
Birthday parties? Yes.

FUN-N-STUFF ACTIVITY CENTER

Did you ever play miniature golf, drive a car, and take a train ride all on the same day? If you think this would be fun to do, take your family to Fun-N-Stuff and do it!

Where is it? At 4800 28th Street in Boulder. Drive north on 28th Street to Lee Hill Road. The Center is on the right side of the road.
Phone number? 442-4386.
Parking? Yes, and it's free.
Open what days and hours? Summers: Mondays through Fridays, 10:30 a.m. to 10:30 p.m.; Saturdays, 10:30 a.m. to midnight; Sundays, noon to midnight. Winters: Mondays through Fridays, 11:00 a.m. to 6:00 p.m.; Saturdays, 10:30 a.m. to 6:00 p.m.; Sundays, noon to 6:00 p.m.
Activities? Three miniature golf courses; kiddie cars; kiddie train ride; one-and two-seater go-carts; batting cages; golf driving range; and a game arcade.
Entrance fees? Charges are made for each ride or activity, ranging from $1.50 to $5.00.
Supervision? No special arrangements are made.
Wheelchair accessible? Yes.
Food? Yes.
Restrooms? Yes.
Birthday parties? Yes.

FUN-PLEX ENTERTAINMENT MALL

Toddlers to teenagers, moms and dads, aunts and uncles, grandmas and grandpas can bounce, crawl, roll, and slide, play video games and Laeserquest, roller skate, bowl, play billiards and miniature golf, and go on rides. Did I leave anyone or anything out?

Where is it? At 9670 West Coal Mine Avenue in Littleton, between Route C-470 and Hampden Avenue.
Phone number? 972-4344.
Parking? Yes, and it's <u>free</u>.
Other transportation? RTD buses stop nearby.
Open what days and hours? Fall, winter, and spring: Mondays through Thursdays, 4:00 p.m. to 10:00 p.m.; Fridays, 4:00 p.m. to 1:00 a.m.; Saturdays, 11:00 a.m. to 1:00 a.m.; Sundays, 11:00 a.m. to 10:00 p.m. Summer: Mondays through Thursdays, 11:00 a.m. to 11:00 p.m.; Fridays, 11:00 a.m. to 1:00 a.m.; Saturdays, 10:00 a.m. to 1:00 a.m.; Sundays, 12 noon to 11:00 p.m.
Admission fees? No general admission charge but there are charges for each activity, ranging from $2.50 to $6.00.
Supervision? Parents are expected to stay with their children.
Wheelchair accessible? Yes.
Food? Yes.
Restrooms? Yes.
Birthday parties? Yes.

JUNGLE JIM'S PLAYLANDS

Do you like riding on a carousel? bumping into cars? spinning like a top? flying in jets? riding on a roller coaster? and climbing in a jungle? If you said yes to one or more of these questions, then you'll enjoy yourself at Jungle Jim's Playlands.

Where are they? **Aurora:** At 13686 East Alameda Avenue and Potomac Street, west of Route I-225 in Aurora; **Arvada:** At 80th Street and Wadsworth Avenue, at the Cubs Food Shopping Center.

Phone numbers? **Aurora:** 360-5333; **Arvada:** 427-3200.

Parking? Yes, and it's free.

Other transportation? RTD buses stop nearby.

Open what days and hours? Both Playlands are open Mondays through Thursdays, 11:00 a.m. to 9:00 p.m.; Fridays and Saturdays, 10:00 a.m. to 10:00 p.m.; Sundays, 11:00 a.m. to 8:00 p.m.; school holidays, 10:00 a.m. to closing.

Admission fees? Children 2 to 18 years old, $4.99 weekdays and $6.99 weekends; children 6 months to 2 years old, $2.99 and $4.99 respectively; infants up to 6 months old and adults, free.

Supervision? Parents are expected to stay with their children.

Wheelchair accessible? Yes.

Food? Yes.

Restrooms? Yes.

Birthday parties? Yes.

KIDSLOPE AT THE CHILDREN'S MUSEUM

Would you like to learn to ski in Denver on an indoor ski slope? Sounds awesome! But you can do it at KidSlope. And when you've learned how to make those boards do what you want them to do and not what they want to do, you can try them out on the majestic, outdoor mountains, covered with real snow. Won't that be cool?

Where is it? At 2121 Children's Museum Drive in Denver. Take Route I-25 to Exit 211 (23rd Avenue) and go east to 7th Street; turn right and right again onto Children's Museum Drive.
Phone number? 433-7444, Extension 121.
Free Parking? Yes.
Other transportation? RTD buses, the Cultural Connection Trolley, and the Platte Valley Trolley stop nearby.
Wheelchair accessible? Yes. Read below about Adaptive Ski Lessons.
Food? Yes.
Restrooms? Yes.

Beginner Ski Lessons
Open what days and hours? Year-round. First-time skiers, children 4 years old and up, are offered lessons from early September through the end of May, on Tuesdays through Fridays at 3:00 p.m., and Saturdays and Sundays at 10:30 a.m., 1:00 p.m., and 3:00 p.m. From June through August, lessons are also given on Mondays at 3:00 p.m. Each lesson lasts for 1½ hours. There are 5 to 9 children in a class.
Lesson fees? $6.00, which includes use of the ski equipment.

Advanced Ski Lessons
Open what days and hours? October through May.
Lesson fees? $38.00, which includes a season pass and the use of ski equipment. After you have three lessons at Kidslope, you receive a day of lessons and skiing at one of several Colorado ski areas at no additional charge. Call and reserve a place at Kidslope before going there.

Adapted Ski Lessons
Open what days and hours? Private lessons for children with special needs offered on six consecutive Tuesday nights.
Lesson fees? $15.00 for all lessons.

OUTDOOR PLAYGROUNDS

The Denver-Boulder metropolitan region has well over 300 parks city-wide and over 50 parks and wilderness areas in the mountains. The facilities may include any of the following, alone or in combination: playing fields, swings, slides, climbing and play equipment, picnic tables, shelters, indoor and outdoor swimming pools, tennis courts, greenbelt trails for walking, biking, and horseback riding, nature centers and preserves, a miniature train ride, a farm, and lakes for boating, fishing, and ice skating. Boating is allowed at some park lakes, by permit only when using your own boat, or you may be able to rent paddle boats, sail boats, or canoes. Fishing is allowed at all park lakes unless a sign says otherwise; children under 15 years old may fish without a license when with a licensed adult. Most parks are free to enter and are open year-round, but fees are charged for special programs and activities, some of which are only offered from the end of May to the beginning of September. Many facilities are accessible by wheelchair. Just a sampling of parks is described below. For more information on parks near you, their facilities, and their year-round and special summer programs call **Denver:** 964-2500 and 697-4545; **Aurora:** 695-7200; **Boulder:** 441-2400, 441-3408, and 441-3950; **Englewood:** 762-2575; **Evergreen:** 674-0532; **Golden:** 279-3331; **Lakewood:** 987-7800; and **Littleton:** 798-2493.

BEAR CREEK LAKE PARK

This Park is amazing. You can bike, walk, or ride a horse; run, play ball, or fly a kite; fish, boat, or smell flowers; count butterflies, hunt animal tracks, or pick up bird feathers; and barbecue, picnic, or camp out. Which will it be?

Where is it? At 15600 West Morrison Road in Lakewood. Drive out Route 6 to the south Kipling Avenue Exit and continue south to Morrison Road. Turn right and just before you come to Route C-470, you'll see the Park entrance on the left-hand side of the road.
Phone numbers? Park, 697-6159; Horseback Riding, 697-1416.
Parking? Yes, and it's <u>free</u>.
Other transportation? No.
Car entrance fees? During the activity season only, senior adults, $1.00 per car; other adults, $2.00 per car.
Wheelchair accessible? Partially.
Food? No.
Restrooms? Yes, the porta-potty variety.

General Use of the Park
Open what days and hours? Year-round, dawn to dusk.

29

Entrance fees? During the Activity Season only, from Memorial Day (end of May) to October 15th.

Bicycling
Trails? In the Park, the bike trail goes around the lake and leads into two other bike trails that go outside the Park.
Bike rentals? $8.00 per hour; or bring your own.
Open what days and hours? Year-round, dawn to dusk.

Horseback Riding
Trails? In the Park.
Open what days and hours? Everyday, Memorial Day to Labor Day (early September), 10:00 a.m. to 7:00 p.m.
Horse rentals? Rent at Old West Stables, located outside the Park entrance. Call 697-1416 for information.

Boating
Open what days and hours? Everyday, Memorial Day to Labor Day, 10:00 a.m. to 7:00 p.m.
Boat rentals? Paddle boats, canoes, and wind surfers, $10.00 an hour; sunfish, $12.00 an hour.

Overnight Camping
Open what days and hours? Everyday, Memorial Day to October 15th.
Camping fees? $6.00 per night.

Related places of interest: Adams County Fair and Rodeo (August); Boulder Reservoir; Boulder Creek Path; Cherry Creek, Platte River, and Highline Canal Greenways; Cherry Creek State Park; Del Mar, Meadowood, Sagebrush, and Utah Parks; Expo Park; National Western Stock Show and Rodeo (January); Washington Park

BELLEVIEW PARK

You can spend a summer's day here, walking on nature trails, cooling your feet in a shallow stream, eating a picnic lunch, playing ball, running on the grass, riding the Lion's Club Train, and petting the animals at the Children's Farm. There are skateboard areas and tennis courts, too. The Train takes you over a wooden trestle, through a tunnel, and around the Children's Farm, where you'll see lambs, pigs, chickens, and a donkey, and you can pet all of them.

Where is it? The east entrance is at 5001 South Inca Street, and the west entrance, at 4800 South Windermere Avenue in Englewood. Drive south on Broadway to Belleview Avenue and turn right. Stay in the far right lane until you reach Inca Avenue, and make a right turn into the Park.

Phone numbers? Park, 762-2575; Farm, 798-6927; Train, 761-1867.

Parking? Yes, and it's <u>free</u>.

Other transportation? RTD buses stop nearby.

Open days and hours? The Park, year-round; the Train and Children's Farm, from Memorial Day (late May) to Labor Day (early September), Tuesdays through Saturdays, 10:00 a.m. to 4:00 p.m.; Sundays, 11:00 a.m. to 4:00 p.m.

Entrance fees? The Park is <u>free</u>. The Train Rides and Children's Farm are <u>free</u> for children under 2; all others pay 50 cents.

Wheelchair accessible? Partially.

Food? No.

Restrooms? Yes.

Related places of interest: Adams County Fair and Rodeo (August); Belmar Park; Colorado Railroad Museum; Denver Zoo Miniature Train Ride; Forney Transportation Museum;

Furry Scurry, Denver Dumb Friends League Benefit (May); Lakeside Amusement Park Miniature Train Ride; Rocky Mountain Pet EXPO (November); Tiny Town Miniature Train Ride; Union Pacific Railroad Station and Model Railroad; National Western Stock Show and Rodeo (January)

BELMAR PARK

You'll like Belmar Park because it has lots of open space for running, flying kites, and catching frisbees. But that's not all. It has two hiking trails, some picnic tables, two lakes, three kinds of water birds, flower gardens, and one great museum! This is a neat place to spend the day.

Belmar Park.
Photo: Lakewood's Historical Belmar Village

Where is it? At 801 South Wadsworth Boulevard, near the Villa Italia Shopping Center, in Belmar Park, Lakewood. Drive west on Route 6 to the South Wadsworth Boulevard exit. Continue south until you come to the Park.
Phone number? 987-7850.
Parking? Yes, and it's free at either the Belmar Museum and Historic Village or the Municipal Building parking lots.
Other transportation? RTD buses stop nearby.
Open what hours and days? Everyday, 8:00 a.m.to 5:00 p.m.
Entrance fees? None. It's free.
Wheelchair accessible? Partially.
Food? At the Municipal Building only.
Restrooms? At the Belmar Museum or Municipal Building.

Related places of interest: Chatfield Arboretum; Denver Botanic Gardens; Lookout Mountain Nature Center: Nature Trails; National Center for Atmospheric Research: Nature Trails

BOULDER CREEK PATH

If you're a jogger, walker, skater, biker, or any combination of these, you'll find nine miles of smooth sailing on the Boulder Creek Path. If you happen to be a naturalist, too, there is much to see. Pine, spruce, cottonwood, and aspen trees grow along the banks and provide homes to many birds, such as chickadees, swallows, robins, flickers, sparrows, jays, magpies, crows, owls, hawks, eagles, and doves. Footprints of sandpiper, raccoon, beaver, muskrat, prairie dog, deer, cougar, and bobcat have been found here. This place is a real treasure!

Where is it? Along the banks of Boulder Creek, between 6th and 28th Streets, in Boulder.
Phone number? 441-3400.
Parking? At various access points along the route, <u>free</u> or metered.
Other transportation? RTD buses stop nearby various access points.
Open what days and hours? Everyday, year-round.
Entrance fees? None. It's <u>free</u>.
Wheelchair accessible? Yes.
Food? No.
Restrooms? No.

Related places of interest: Bald Eagle Days (January); Barr State Park Bird Banding; Daniels Park Wildlife Preserve; Genesee Park; HawkQuest; HawkWatch and Count; National Center for Atmospheric Research: Nature Preserve; Rocky Mountain Arsenal National Wildlife Refuge; Settlers Park and Boulder Creek Path Bird Walks

BOULDER RESERVOIR

The great thing about this Park is that they will teach you to boat and water ski if you want to learn. But, if that doesn't interest you, maybe you'd just like to cool off from the hot summer sun by swimming in the lake and then try to catch your dinner by fishing. All is possible at Boulder Reservoir.

Where is it? At 5100 North 51st Street in Longmont. Drive east on the Foothills Highway to the Longmont Diagonal. Take Colorado Route 119 to Jay Road where you'll see a sign to Boulder Reservoir. Drive out Jay Road to 51st Street,

turn right and drive 1½ miles to the Reservoir's front gate.
Phone numbers? 441-3461 or 441-3400.
Parking? Yes, and it's <u>free</u>.
Other transportation? No.
Wheelchair accessible? Yes.
Food? Yes, from Memorial Day (end of May) to Labor Day (early September).
Restrooms? Yes.

General Use of the Park
Open what days and hours? Year-round, dawn to dusk.
Entrance fees? After Labor Day to Memorial Day, it's <u>free</u>. Memorial Day to Labor Day: Children 5 years old and younger, <u>free</u>; 6 to 12 year-olds and senior adults 65 and older, $1.50; 13 to 18 year-olds, $2.25; 19 to 64 year-olds, $3.50. If you just plan on fishing, avoid the front gate and drive to the Water Treatment Plant on 63rd Street, park <u>free</u> any time, and walk to the dam. No entrance fee.

Swimming
Open what days and hours? Memorial Day to Labor Day only, 9:30 a.m. to 6:30 p.m.
Lessons? No.

Boating
Open what days and hours? Memorial Day to Labor Day only, Tuesdays and Thursdays, 9:00 a.m. to dusk; Mondays, Wednesdays, Fridays and weekends, dawn to dusk.
Entrance fees? None. It's <u>free</u>.
Boat rentals? You can bring your own boat or rent one by the hour: row boats, canoes, paddle boats, $5; sailboats, $10.00; jet boats, $20.00.
Lessons? Boating and water skiing. Call for brochure, 441-3400.

Fishing

Open what days and hours? Year-round, dawn to dusk.
Entrance fees? None. It's <u>free</u>.
Fishing license? Not needed for children up to 15 years old when accompanied by a licensed adult.

**Related places of interest:** Bear Creek Lake Park; Cherry Creek State Park; Evergreen Lake Park

CHATFIELD ARBORETUM

Hiking through beautiful, quiet, forested trails, past beaver dams and lakes with geese and ducks, is a terrific way to spend the day. You can run, romp, and roll or snoop, sniff, and sneak-up on the birds, bees, and flowers along the trails. Bring along a picnic, too. And, before you leave, stop in at the Visitor's Center to see the animals and flowers, or go to the Nature Center to see bees making honey. What a sweet place to bee!

Where is it? 9201 South Carr Street in Littleton.
Phone number? 973-3705.
Parking? Yes, and it's <u>free</u>.
Other transportation? No.
Open what days and hours? April 1st to October 31st, everyday, 9:00 a.m. to 5:00 p.m.; remainder of the year, Mondays through Saturdays, 9:00 a.m. to 5:00 p.m.; closed Sundays and holidays.
Entrance fees? Children are <u>free</u>; adults, $1.00.
Trail information? At the Visitor's Center.
Wheelchair accessible? Yes. All trails are asphalted.
Food? Yes.

Restrooms? Yes.

Related places of interest: *Bear Creek Lake Park; Belmar Park; Denver Botanic Gardens*

CHAUTAUQUA PARK

Next time someone says, "Go take a hike," head for Chautauqua Park. It's a hiker's paradise. There are miles of carefully-marked hiking trails that range from easy to extremely difficult. Some of them link up with trails at the National Center for Atmospheric Research. In addition to hiking trails, there are outstanding geological sites, too, such as Royal Arch, Woods Quarry, Tomato Rock, Mallory Cave, and Saddle Rock. These are no ordinary hiking trails. Bring a day-pack, water, and trail snacks and hit those trails!

Where is it? West on Baseline Road to 9th Street in Boulder. The Park is on the left side of the street.
Phone number? 441-3408.
Parking? Yes, and it's <u>free</u> in the parking lots and on the street.
Other transportation? RTD buses stop nearby.
Open what days and hours? Everyday, all day, dawn to dusk.
Entrance fees? None. It's <u>free</u>.
Trail information? Yes, from Boulder County Parks and Open Space Ranger Station.
Wheelchair accessible? Partially.
Food? No.
Restrooms? Yes.

Related places of interest: *Dakota Hogback Geological Cross-Section Site; Daniels Park Trails; Dinosaur Ridge Tours; Genesee Park; Geology Museum; Denver Museum of Natural History; Lookout Mountain Nature Center: Nature Trails; National Center for Atmospheric Research: Nature Trails; Genesee Park*

CHERRY CREEK. PLATTE RIVER, AND HIGHLINE CANAL GREENWAYS

What a treat! You can ride your trike or bike, walk or run, and even skate on these paved trails for miles and miles all year-round! And they run along a pretty creek, a trolley track, and a narrow canal. If you look carefully along Cherry Creek and the Highline Canal, you'll see many different kinds of birds, those that fly and those that swim, as well as other little creatures scampering around. The Platte River Greenway provides an entirely different view, one of smoke stacks and sky scrapers, and of the roller coaster and ferris wheel at the new Elitch Gardens Amusement Park.

Where are they? They're in Denver. Cherry Creek Greenway extends from Quebec Street to Confluence Park, where it intersects the Platte River Greenway, covering a distance of approximately 8 miles. The Platte River Greenway extends from the north to the south city limits, approximately 11½ miles, and there are nature and historic information plaques posted along the way. The Highline Canal covers the area from Hampden to Virginia Avenues, about 16 miles.

The Greenways can be accessed from many points along their routes. For example, the Cherry Creek Greenway may be accessed downtown, off Speer Boulevard and Larimer Street, and in east Denver, off First Avenue or on the south side of the Cherry Creek Mall. For more information, request a map from Denver Parks.

Phone number? 698-4011.

Parking? At various points along the route, <u>free</u> or metered.

Other transportation? RTD buses stop at various points along the route.

Open what days and hours? Everyday, all day.

Entrance fees? None. It's <u>free</u>.

Wheelchair accessible? Yes, from some ramps that meet the grade limitations.

Food? No.

Restrooms? No.

Related places of interest: Boulder Creek Path

CHERRY CREEK STATE PARK

Cherry Creek State Park includes a large lake (reservoir) used by swimmers at the swimming beach, by boaters at the marina, and by fisher-girls and boys from the edge of the lake or from a boat. There are plenty of picnic tables and, if overnight camping sounds good to you, you can do that here as well. If you're looking for trail action, take a hike, ride a bike, or "get up on your high horse." The Painted Horse Stables rents horses to you if you are 7 years old or older. They'll teach you how to ride, or you can just take a bouncy walk on the trail, with a guide riding alongside.

Where is it? At 4201 South Parker Road in Aurora.

Phone numbers? General information, 690-1166; boating,

794-6144; swimming, 699-3871; fishing, 690-1166 Extension 2; horseback riding, 690-8235; overnight camping, 690-1166, Extension 4.

Parking? Yes and it's <u>free</u>.
Other transportation? RTD buses stop nearby.
Park entrance fee? $4.00 per car.
Wheelchair accessible? Partially.
Food? Yes.
Restrooms? Yes.

General Use of the Park
Open what days and hours? Summers, every day, 5:00 a.m. to 10:00 p.m.; winters: every day, 6:00 a.m. to 7:00 p.m.

Boating
Open what days and hours? Mid-April to Memorial Day (late May) and Labor Day (early September) to mid-October, 8:00 a.m. to 8:00 p.m.; Memorial Day to Labor Day, 10:00 a.m. to 6:00 p.m.
Bring you own? Yes, but a permit is required.
Boat rental? Canoes, paddle boats, row boats, each $10.00 per hour plus a refundable $25.00 deposit; motorized fishing boats, $20.00 per hour plus a refundable $25.00 deposit; speedboats and pontoon boats, $45.00 an hour plus a refundable deposit.

Swimming
Open what days and hours? Memorial Day (end of May) to Labor Day (beginning of September), 7:00 a.m. to 10:00 p.m. A life-guard is on duty from 8:00 a.m. to 6:00 p.m. only.

Fishing
Open what days and hours? Memorial Day (end of May) to

Labor Day (beginning of September), 7:00 a.m. to 10:00 p.m. The Lake is stocked each year and fishing is very popular here.

Fishing license? None needed for children up to 15 years <u>old</u>, but child must be with a licensed adult.

Horseback Riding
Horse trails? In the Park.

Open what days and hours? Year-round, everyday, weather permitting. Cold weather days, weekends only. When in doubt, call.

Horse rental? $14.00 per hour; $20.00 per 1½ hours; $26.00 per 2 hours.

Overnight Camping
Open what days and hours? Everyday, April through October.

Rental? $7.00 per night.

Related places of interest: *Adams County Fair and Rodeo (August); Bear Creek Lake Park; Boulder Reservoir; National Western Stock Show and Rodeo (January)*

CRAMNER PARK

Would you like to see a whole mountain range at one time? Would you like to know the names of those mountains and find out how high they are? If you said yes-yes, then go to Cramner Park on a bright, clear day any time of the year. From a stone platform, you'll see famous Pike's Peak to the south, majestic Mount Evans straight ahead, and fabulous Long's Peak to the north...as well as all the other marvelous mountains in between. Along the edge of the platform, each mountain is drawn in stone, with its name and height placed below it.

The Park is also called Sun Dial Park. You won't need a wrist watch to tell you the time as long as the sun is out. After seeing the mountains and the sun dial, you might like to run around on the grass, play catch or tag, or maybe even fly a kite if the wind is strong enough. There's a drinking fountain on the south side of the platform, just in case you need to wet your whistle.

Where is it? At First and Third Avenues and Clermont and Ash Streets in Denver. Drive east on Sixth Avenue, past Colorado Boulevard to Clermont Street and turn right. Continue for three more blocks to the Park.

Phone number? 964-2581.

Parking? Yes, and it's <u>free</u>.

Other transportation? RTD buses stop nearby.

Wheelchair accessible? Yes.

Food? No.

Restrooms? No.

Related places of interest: Del Mar, Meadowood, Sagebrush, and Utah Parks; Expo Park; Genesee Park; Washington Park

DANIELS PARK TRAILS

There are over 1,000 acres of land in this Park. Bring your day pack with lunch, snacks, water, a compass, and binoculars, and hike the trails in the 40 acres open to you. Don't miss one of the greatest views around, the one overlooking the plains and mountains.

And that's not all. There is a preserve for 50 buffalo kept within a large fenced-in area. The big, brawny buffalos, with their shaggy hair, curved horns, and humped back, may be seen from the road that cuts through the park and borders their grazing land. If you're very quiet and a good detective, you may see some elk, antelope, deer, wild turkey, coyote, and perhaps a colony of prairie dogs. Keep alert and use your binoculars to hunt them down. Good luck, detectives!

Where is it? On Daniels Park Road in Sedalia. Take Route I-25 south to either Lincoln Avenue or Castle Pines Exits. Drive south approximately three miles to the Park.
Phone number? 660-9853.
Parking? Yes, and it's free.
Other transportation? No.
Open what days and hours? Daily, 5:00 a.m. to 11:00 p.m.
Wheelchair accessible? No.
Food? No.
Restrooms? Yes, the out-house variety.

Related places of interest: Genesee Park; National Western Stock Show and Rodeo (January); Rocky Mountain Arsenal National Wildlife Refuge

DEL MAR, MEADOWOOD, SAGEBRUSH, AND UTAH PARKS

Are you tired of "oweys" and "boo-boos," scratches and scrapes, bumps and bruises? It's time you played in these Aurora Parks where soft, bouncy cushions of rubber have replaced the cement and gravel placed beneath the slides, swings, and jungle gyms of most playgrounds.

Each Park has many other things for you to use, such as bike trails, ball fields, and picnic tables. Del Mar and Utah Parks also have swimming pools (indoors or outdoors), and Utah Park has a fishing lake, and racquetball and tennis courts. Maybe the exercise path at Utah Park will get you in shape; or the nature area at Meadowood Park will give you ideas for your next science project. Meadowood Park also has a year-round Recreation Center. Find out which Park is your favorite.

Where are they? They are all in Aurora. Del Mar Park is at 12000 East Sixth Avenue and Peoria Street. Drive east on Alameda Avenue to Peoria Street and turn left. Continue on to Sixth Avenue. Meadowood Park is at 16225 East Dartmouth Avenue, between Chambers and Buckley Roads Drive east on Alameda Avenue to Chambers Road. Turn right and continue to East Dartmouth Avenue and turn left to Buckley Road. Sagebrush Park is at 4744 South Evanston Way, between Quincy and Belleview Avenues. Drive east on Alameda Avenue to Chambers Road, turn right and continue past Quincy Avenue to the Park. Utah Park is at 1800 South Peoria Street, near Jewell Avenue. Then drive east on Alameda Avenue to Peoria Street. Turn right and continue past Jewell Avenue to the Park.

Phone number? 695-7200.

Parking? Yes, and it's <u>free</u>.

Other transportation? RTD buses stop nearby.

Open what days and hours? Dawn to dusk, year-round.

Entrance fees? None. It's <u>free</u>.

Recreation center? Utah, yes; Del Mar, Meadowood, and Sagebrush Parks, no.

Wheelchair accessible? Del Mar and Utah Parks, yes; Meadowood Park, partially; Sagebrush Park, no.

Food? No.
Restrooms? Del Mar Park, yes; Meadowood, Sagebrush, and Utah Parks, no.

Related places of interest: Bear Creek Lake Park; Boulder Creek Path; Boulder Reservoir; Cherry Creek State Park; Cherry Creek, Platte River, and Highline Canal Greenways; Expo Park; School Playgrounds; Washington Park

EVERGREEN LAKE PARK

Would you like to ice skate on a beautiful lake some brisk winter's day in sunlight or at night by lamp-light? And how about taking a hike around the lake, fishing, or going out in a paddle boat some sunny summer's day? Winter or summer, plan a visit to Evergreen Lake Park!

Where is it? At 29614 Upper Bear Creek Road in Evergreen. Drive west on Route I-70 to the El Rancho Exit. Then, take Route 74 into Evergreen. When you reach the only stop light in Evergreen, drive a half-mile and take a left turn onto Bear Creek Road.
Phone numbers? 674-2677 or 674-0532.
Parking? Yes, and it's <u>free</u>, but the parking lot cannot accommodate all comers. Be prepared to park up to a mile away some days.
Other transportation? No.
Wheelchair accessible? Partially.
Food? Yes, when the activities are open.
Restrooms? Yes.

Ice Skating
Open what days and hours? As soon as it's cold enough and for as long as the Lake stays frozen; Mondays to Fridays, 4:00 p.m. to 7:00 p.m.; Saturdays and Sundays, 10:00 a.m. to 7:00 p.m.; December 18th to January 1st, 10:00 a.m. to 7:00 p.m.; limited hours on Christmas' eve, Christmas day, New Year's eve, and New Year's day. Wheelchairs are permitted on the ice.
Entrance fees? Children 12 and under and senior adults, $1.50; 13 to 18 year-olds, $1.75; other adults, $2.00.
Skate rental? $2.00 an hour.

Boating
Open what days and hours? In the summer, every good-weather day from Memorial Day (the end of May) to Labor Day (the beginning of September), 10:00 a.m. to 6:00 p.m.
Entrance fees? None. It's free.
Boat rental? Paddle boats, $4.00 per ½ hour; canoes, $5.00 per hour. A deposit of $5.00 and a picture identification are required.

Fishing
Open what days and hours? Memorial Day to Labor Day, every good-weather day.
Fishing fees? No. It's free.
Fishing license? None for children under 15 years old but they must be with a licensed adult.

Hiking
Open what days and hours? Everyday, year-round, dawn to dusk.
Entrance fees? None. It's free.

Related places of interest: Bear Creek Lake Park; Boulder Reservoir; Cherry Creek State Park; Evergreen Lake Park; Expo Park

EXPO PARK

This is a neat place to spend a day, moving from the playground to the bike trail, the volleyball, football, and soccer fields, and to the tennis and basketball courts. Don't forget to bring your fishing pole, tackle box, and bait because there's a fishing pond as well. When its time to eat your fish, you'll find barbecue grills and picnic tables. Yummy! Be sure to bring along water and other drinkables.

Where is it? At 11001 East Exposition Avenue in Aurora. Drive east on Sixth Avenue to Peoria Street and turn left. The Park is located between Alameda and Mississippi Avenues.
Phone number? 695-7200.
Parking? Yes, and it's free.
Other transportation? Yes. RTD buses stop nearby.
Open what days and hours? Everyday, year-round.
Entrance fees? No. It's free.
Recreation center? Yes.
Wheelchair accessible? Partially.
Food? No.
Restrooms? No.

Related places of interest: Boulder Creek Path; Cherry Creek, Platte River, and Highline Canal Greenways; Del Mar, Meadowood, Sagebrush, and Utah Parks; Washington Park

GENESEE PARK

If you like being in the mountains but don't like to drive in the car for too long, then Genesee Park is the place to go. You can hike on three good trails: the Beaver Brook Trail, the Chavez Trail, and a braille trail for those of you who are visually impaired. Bring along a butterfly net, bug jars, and a magnifying glass to make the hike more interesting. You might want to keep a look-out for roaming elk and deer and other four-legged creatures running about the Park with you.

The playing field is great, too, for catching balls or frisbees. And when you're tired and hungry, set out your picnic on one of the tables and take a lunch break.

When you're finished playing and eating, you might want to visit the buffalo and elk herds nearby in the fenced-in areas at Genesee Park Buffalo and Elk Ranch. Walk along the loop trail around the edge of the Park where they are likely to be grazing. They are awesome!

Where is it? It's off Route I-70 at Exit 254, 20 miles west of Denver in Golden.
Phone number? 526-1550.
Parking? Yes, and it's <u>free</u>.
Other transportation? RTD buses stop nearby.
Entrance fees? None. It's <u>free</u>.
Wheelchair accessible? Partially.
Food? No.
Restrooms? Yes.

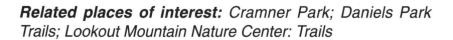

Related places of interest: *Cramner Park; Daniels Park Trails; Lookout Mountain Nature Center: Trails*

LOOKOUT MOUNTAIN NATURE CENTER: NATURE TRAILS

Do you like to discover things? The Nature Trails at Lookout Mountain Nature Center are filled with things to discover while you walk along the Trails. You'll see animal tracks; you'll sniff out wild flowers; you'll sight low-flying birds; and you'll unearth creepy-crawly spiders and insects...for starters. Walk along the Nature Trails with wide-open eyes and ears and an alert nose so you won't miss a thing! Bring along water and a trail snack to keep up your energy so you can continue on the trails that connect you with nearby parks.

Where is it? At 910 Colorow Road in Golden, at the top of Lookout Mountain. Drive west on Route I-70 and take Exit 256. It's a five-minute drive from there. Follow the brown and white signs to the Jefferson County Conference and Nature Center.

Phone numbers? 526-0594; hearing impaired, 271-5926.

Parking? Yes, and it's <u>free</u>.

Other transportation? No.

Open what days and hours? Trails are open daily, 8:00 a.m. to dusk. The Center is open Tuesdays through Sundays, 10:00 a.m. to 4:00 p.m.

Trails? There is a self-guided nature trail and trail-links to other parks in the area.

Wheelchair accessible? Yes, but the trails exceed maximum grade.

Fees? None. It's <u>free</u>.

Food? No.

Restrooms? Yes, in the Nature Center building which is open between 10:00 a.m. and 4:00 p.m.

Related places of interest: *Chautauqua Park; Daniels Park Trails and Wildlife Preserve; Genesee Park; Meadowood Park; National Center for Atmospheric Research; Rocky Mountain Arsenal National Wildlife Refuge*

NATIONAL CENTER FOR ATMOSPHERIC RESEARCH (NCAR): NATURE TRAILS

If you're into hiking and breathtaking views of Boulder and the Great Plains, you'll enjoy the many well-kept trails here. The Walter Orr Roberts Mesa Nature Trail is a ¼-mile loop trail which is wheelchair accessible. The other trails range from easy to very difficult. Some of them link up with trails in Chautauqua Park so you can cover a lot of ground. Don't forget your binoculars to bring the views, the birds, and the deer closer. And, if you want to make those little creepy crawly caterpillars, beetles, and teeny-tiny insects into friendly giants, use a magnifying glass! Bring along trail snacks and plenty of water. They'll taste great and keep you feeling great at the same time!

Where is it? At West Table Mesa Drive in south-western Boulder. Drive south on Broadway to the South Boulder Road, turn right and continue out to when it becomes Table Mesa Drive. Stay on Table Mesa Drive to the NCAR parking lot.
Phone number? 441-3950.
Parking? Yes, and it's free.
Other transportation? RTD buses stop nearby but infrequently. Call 443-0100 for times.
Open what days? Everyday, all year-round.
Entrance fees? None. It's free.

Mule Deer.
Photo: National Center for Atmospheric Research/UCAR/NSF

Trail information? At the kiosk in NCAR's lobby.
Wheelchair accessible? Partially: the Walter Orr Roberts Mesa Nature Trail and NCAR's building.
Food? Yes, in NCAR's cafeteria, Mondays through Fridays, 8:00
Restrooms? Yes, in NCAR's lobby.

Related places of interest: Chatfield Arboretum; Chautauqua Park; Daniels Park Trails; Genesee Park; Lookout Mountain Nature Center; Meadowood Park

SCHOOL PLAYGROUNDS

As you drive or walk by a School Playground, take a good look at the playing fields, swings, slides, climbing equipment, and tennis courts. If it looks like a place where you'd like to play and there isn't a locked fence around it, then you can use the playground after school hours, on weekends, and during school holidays.

Where are they? In your neighborhood.
Phone number? Check you phone directory for your school district information number.
Parking? Yes, and it's <u>free</u>.
Other transportation? Call RTD for information.
Wheel chair accessible? Call school district information.
Food? No.
Restrooms? No.

Related places of interest: Del Mar, Meadowood, Sagebrush, and Utah Parks, Expo Park

WASHINGTON PARK

This is the biggest and busiest park in the city of Denver. You can bike, skate, jog, and drive your wheelchair on lots of closed-off roadways year-round. On weekends, people play basketball, football, soccer and volleyball. The tennis courts are busy, too. If you have a row boat, canoe, or kayak, and a life jacket and boat permit, you can row, paddle and skim around the lake.

Did you know that the Park people stock the pond with fish each year in the northeast corner of the park? Only children under 15 years old are allowed to fish here.

If you'd like to learn about the finer points of fishing, such as how to rig up your fishing pole, and how to cast your line to the hungry fish, then sign up for the Fishing Clinic. Not only will you be the greatest, safest, and most thoughtful fisher-person ever, but you'll also get the pole, tackle, and tackle box for your very own!

Where is it? The Park extends east and west between South Franklin and South Downing Streets, and is bordered on the north and south by Ohio and Louisiana Avenues in Denver. Drive east on Alameda Avenue to South Franklin Street, turn right, and continue to the Park.

Phone numbers? General information, 698-4011; boating, 964-2522; fishing, 698-4962; Recreation Center, 698-4962.

Parking? Yes, and it's <u>free</u>.

Other transportation? RTD buses stop nearby.

Open what days and hours? Everyday, year-round.

Recreation center? Yes.

Wheelchair accessible? Partially.

Food? No.

Restrooms? Yes.

Boating
Open what days? Everyday, year-round.

Boat rentals? No. Bring your own boat with a permit.

Entrance fees? No, it's <u>free</u>.

Fishing
Where? At the pond, next to the fire station at Franklin Street and Virginia Avenue.

Open what days? Everyday, year-round.

Fishing fees? No, it's <u>free</u> for children up to 15 years old.

Fishing clinic? Yes, and it's <u>free</u>.

Related places of interest: *Bear Creek Lake Park; Boulder Creek Path; Boulder Reservoir; Cherry Creek, Platte River, and Highline Canal Greenways; Cherry Creek State Park; Evergreen Lake Park*

AMUSEMENT PARKS

ELITCH GARDENS AMUSEMENT PARK

The new Elitches is due to open in the spring of 1995. The original Park was over 100 years old when it closed down in the fall of 1994. It was known for its beautiful gardens and many exciting rides. The new Elitch Gardens promise to be even better. It will be twice as big and beautiful as the old Park, with rides, games, and activities for kids of all ages.

Where will it be? Across from the Children's Museum and Mile High Stadium. Call for driving directions. *Exit 212A - Speer Blvd. So*
Phone number? ~~455-4771.~~ *595- 4386*
Parking? Yes, and it will be <u>free</u>.
Other transportation? RTD buses, the Cultural Connection Trolley, and the Platte Valley Trolley stop nearby.
Open what days and hours? Call for this information.
Entrance fees? Call for this information
Wheelchair accessible? Yes.
Food? Yes.
Restrooms? Yes.
Birthday parties? Yes.

Related places of interest: *Adams County Fair and Rodeo (August); Buffalo Bill Days (July); Heritage Square; Lakeside Amusement Park; Rocky Mountain River Festival (June)*

HERITAGE SQUARE

If you could take a trip in a Time Machine back to the 1860s, you'd be seeing covered wagons lumbering westward instead of cars and trucks speeding by Heritage Square. This is the same road people used over 130 years ago!

Walking around Heritage Square will help you imagine what a western town looked like in the old days. There are lots of shops, each selling something different. But be sure to save some money for the Alpine and Water Slides, the Bungee Tower, the Rapid Riser, the Trampoline, and the Kiddie Rides. And don't forget the Music Hall where they perform children's theater, play music, present a melodrama, and serve dinner. Then there's a Western music show at the Lazy H Chuckwagon, where you can get dinner the old-fashioned, cowboy way, by standing in line.

Where is it? At 18301 West Colfax in Golden, at the intersection of Route 40 and Sixth Avenue. Drive west on Route I-70 and take Exit 259. Drive north about one mile.
Phone numbers? General: 279-2789; Alpine and Water Slides, 279-1661; Bungee Tower, Rapid Riser, and Trampoline, 279-1661; Children's Theater: 279-7800; Kiddie Amusements: 271-9198; Lazy H Chuckwagon, 278-1938; Music Hall, 279-7800.
Parking? Yes, and it's <u>free</u>.
Other transportation? No.

Entrance fees? No general admission charge, but there are fees for individual activities.
Wheelchair accessible? Partially.
Food? Yes.
Restrooms? Yes.

The Village
Open what days and hours? Memorial Day (late May) to Labor Day (early September), Mondays through Saturdays, 10:00 a.m. to 9:00 p.m.; Sundays, 11:00 a.m. to 9:00 p.m.

Kiddie Amusements
Open what days and hours? Memorial Day to Labor Day, everyday, 10:00 a.m. to 9:00 p.m.
Entrance fees? Each ride or activity, between one and five tickets: one ticket, $1.00; 10 tickets, $9.50, and 20 tickets, $17.50.
Requirements? Age and/or height are specific for each ride.

Alpine Slide
Open what days and hours? Memorial Day to Labor Day, everyday, 10:00 a.m. to 9:00 p.m.
Entrance fees? Junior single ride, $3.00; adult single ride, $4.00.

Water Slide
Open what days and hours? Memorial Day to Labor Day, everyday, 11:00 a.m. to 5:00 p.m.
Entrance fees? Unlimited rides and pool time, $5.00.

Bungee Tower, Rapid Riser, and Trampoline
Open what days and hours? Memorial Day to Labor Day, everyday, noon to 9:00 p.m.

Entrance fees? Bungee Tower, $20.00 per jump; Rapid Riser, $10.00 per ride; Trampoline, $3.00 per turn.
Requirement? Bungee Tower: must weigh 80 pounds or more.

Children's Theater
See description in Chapter 5, under Heritage Square Children's Theatre, page 173.

Related places of interest: Adams County Fair and Rodeo (August); Buffalo Bill Days (July); Elitch Gardens Amusement Park; Lakeside Amusement Park; Hyland Hills Water World; Rocky Mountain River Festival (June); Southshore Water Park

HYLAND HILLS WATER WORLD

Do you love swimming and playing games in the water? Would you like to scream your way down the Screaming Meany Slide, or discover the thrills coasting down one of the other 29 slides? There is water, water everywhere, including two large wave pools, a water fall, raging rivers, and inner-tube rapids. If you are three years old or younger, there's Wally's World for Kids. And for you older guys, there's Calypso Cove, Voyage to the Center of the Earth, River Country, Lazy River, Lost River of the Pharos, Thrill Hill, Thunder Bay, and the Bermuda Triangle...plenty of watery adventures for all!

Where is it? At 88th Avenue at Pecos Street in Westminster. Take Route I-25 Exit 219 (84th Avenue) and drive west on 84th Avenue to Pecos Street. Turn right and continue to 88th Avenue.

Phone number? 427-7873.
Parking? Yes, and it's <u>free</u>.
Other transportation? RTD buses stop nearby.
Open what days and hours? Every good-weather day, Memorial Day (late May) to Labor Day (early September), 10:00 a.m. to 6:00 p.m.
Entrance fees? <u>Free</u> admission for children 3 and under and for senior adults; 4 to 12 year-olds, $13.95; other adults, $14.95; residents of Hyland Hills and Westminster, with identification cards, $5.50 for children, $6.50 for adults. Half-day rates start at 3:30 p.m.
Supervision? Life Guards are situated at each of the water activities.
Wheelchair accessible? Yes.
Food? Yes.
Restrooms? Yes.
Birthday parties? Yes.

Hyland Hills Water World.
Photo: Hyland Hills Water World

LAKESIDE AMUSEMENT PARK

What would the largest amusement park in the Rocky Mountain region look like? As of this writing, it's Lakeside, believe it or not! It's big and that means there are amusements galore for children of all ages. There are fifteen daring kiddie rides as well as a scenic miniature Train Ride. For those of you who are older, braver, and bolder, there's the amazing Cyclone Roller Coaster as well as 40 other rides and many, many games to play.

Lakeside Amusement Park.

Photo: Lakeside Amusement Park

Where is it? At Route I-70 and Sheridan Boulevard in Arvada.

Phone number? 477-1621.

Parking? Yes, and it's <u>free</u>.

Other transportation? RTD buses stop nearby.

Open what days and hours? Late April to late May, weekends only: Fridays, 6:00 to 11:00 p.m.; Saturdays and Sundays, noon to 11:00 p.m. Memorial Day (late May) to Labor Day (early September), Kiddie Land, Mondays to Fridays, 12:30 to 10:00 p.m.; Saturdays and Sundays, noon to 11:00 p.m.; Other rides, Mondays to Fridays, 6:00 p.m. to 11:00 p.m.; Saturdays and Sundays, noon to 11:00 p.m.

Entrance fees? $1.50 for everyone plus the cost of the rides.

Activity fees? An unlimited ride pass, $8.75, for all ages; or ride coupons at 25 cents each, with rides costing between two and five coupons.

Wheelchair accessible? Yes.

Food? Yes.

Restrooms? Yes.

Related places of interest: Adams County Fair and Rodeo (August); Buffalo Bill Days (July); Elitch Gardens Amusement Park; Heritage Square; Rocky Mountain River Festival (June); Tiny Town

SOUTHSHORE WATER PARK

Would you like to make a big splash? Try the water slides. There are two speed slides and four body slides. Or maybe you'd just like to make waves. If so, there's a wave pool. You'll see water, water everywhere...even for toddlers.

There are shady areas, too. It's a cool place to spend a hot summer's day.

Where is it? 10750 East Briarwood Avenue in Englewood. Drive south on Route I-25 and take the Arapahoe Road Exit. Continue east one mile to Havana Avenue, turn right and Southshore Water Park is one block down the road.
Phone number? 649-9875.
Parking? Yes, and it's <u>free</u>.
Other transportation? RTD buses stop nearby on Arapahoe Road.
Open what days and hours? Everyday, mid-May to mid-September, 10:00 a.m. to 6:00 p.m.
Entrance fees? Children, $9.95; adults, $10.95.
Supervision? Life Guards are positioned at each of the activities.
Wheelchair accessible? Yes.
Food? Yes.
Restrooms? Yes.
Birthday parties? Yes.

Related places of interest: Heritage Square; Hyland Hills Water World

TINY TOWN

Have you seen the picture storybook, *The Little Engine That Could*? If you have and you think all trains should look like that one, you'll jump with joy when you see the miniature steam engine and train at Tiny Town. The train's engine puffs smoke as it chugs along a one-mile track that passes by one hundred tiny hand-made buildings that look just like full-sized ones. Best of all, you can be a passenger on that train. Though the train doesn't go over a huge mountain like the storybook train does, you can almost imagine the engine saying, "I know I could if I had to; I know I could."

Where is it? At 6249 South Turkey Creek Road in Evergreen. Drive west on U.S. Route 285, past the Parmilee Gulch interchange. Turn left onto South Turkey Creek Road and continue on this road for half a mile. Tiny Town is on the right side of the road.

What is it? This is the oldest kid-sized village in the United States. It has an authentic coal-fired steam-engine pulling a miniature train one-mile around the one hundred hand-made buildings that make up the town.

Phone numbers? 790-9393 or 697-6829.

Parking? Yes, and it's <u>free</u>.

Other transportation? No.

Open what days and hours? Daily, June through September, 10:00 a.m. to 5:00 p.m. Weekends, May and October, 10:00 a.m. to 4:00 p.m.

Entrance fees? Children, $1.00; adults, $2.00.

Train ride fees? $1.00.

Wheelchair accessible? Yes.

Food? Yes.

Restrooms? Yes.

Birthday parties? Yes.

Related places of interest: Colorado Railroad Museum; Forney Transportation Museum; Denver Zoo Miniature Train Ride; Lakeside Amusement Park's Miniature Train Ride; Lion's Club Train Ride at Belleview Park; Model Railroad at the Union Pacific Railroad Station

Tiny Town.

Photo: Tiny Town

CHAPTER 3

Watching Wildlife: Animals of Colorado and from around the World

Animals have a special place of importance in our lives. They are wonderful companions as pets, but they also provide us with important products, such as clothes, food, and fertilizer. In addition, many animals continue to work for us as hunters, herders, protectors, and entertainers. By observing animals, we have learned a great deal about ourselves and about how to take care of ourselves better. We also have learned that animals help to keep our planet healthy and that we need to protect them, too.

In Denver and the surrounding area, we are fortunate to have quite a few animals that we can observe in their natural

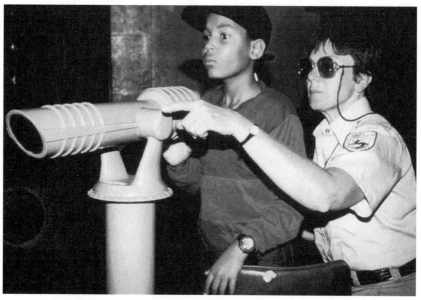

Wildlife spotting at the Rocky Mountain Arsenal.
Photo: Rocky Mountain Arsenal National Wildlife Refuge by
Wendy Shattil & Rob Rozinski

settings. Many of these places are described below. In addition, we have a wonderful zoo which continues to develop the very best facilities for animals from around the world. As you will discover, it's the next best thing to going on a safari to the plains of Africa, the rain forests of South America, and the mountains of Tibet. It would be fun keeping a record of all the animals you see. You could draw pictures of them or take pictures with a camera and come up with your own animal alphabet book.

ANIMALS OF COLORADO

BARR LAKE STATE PARK BIRD BANDING

Have you ever seen a bird with a band on its leg? Did you wonder how it got there, who did it, and why it was done? You can get answers to these important questions by going to Barr State Park during the fall months. That's where the Colorado Bird Observatory does this work and they may let you help them.

Where is it? 13401 Picadilly Road in Brighton. Drive north on Route I-25 and exit to Route I-76, heading east. Then take Exit 22 to Bromley Lane, turn right and continue on to Picadilly Road. The Park entrance is 2 miles down this road.
Phone number? 659-4348, the Colorado Bird Observatory.
Parking? Yes, and it's free.
Other transportation? No.
Open what days and hours? Late August to early November, 7:00 to 11:30 a.m. Call for dates and information on where to meet.

Entrance Fees? $3.00 to enter the Park; the program is free.
Wheelchair accessible? In dry weather only.
Food? No.
Restrooms? Yes.

Related places of interest: Bald Eagle Days (January); Cherry Creek, Platte River, and Highline Canal Greenways; HawkQuest; HawkWatch and Count; Rocky Mountain Arsenal National Wildlife Refuge; Settlers Park and Boulder Creek Path Bird Walks

BELLEVIEW PARK CHILDREN'S FARM

Would you like to see real farm animals? Go to the Children's Farm in Belleview Park. As soon as you see these cute, cuddly creatures, you're probably going to want to pet a lamb, hug a piglet, and tickle a chicken. No one will say, "Don't touch the animals." Instead, you'll be told it's okay; just be gentle when you do.

Where is it? At 5001 South Inca Avenue in Englewood, in Belleview Park. Drive south on Broadway to Belleview Avenue and turn right. Stay in the far right lane until you reach Inca Avenue and turn right into the Park.
Phone number? 798-6927.
Parking? Yes, and it's free.
Other transportation? RTD buses stop nearby.
Open what days and hours? Memorial Day (late May) to Labor Day (early September), Tuesdays through Sundays, 9:00 a.m. to 4:00 p.m.
Entrance Fees? Children under 2 years old, free; all others, 50 cents.

Wheelchair accessible? Yes.
Food? No.
Restrooms? Yes.

Related places of interest: Adams County Fair and Rodeo (August); Channel 4 Education EXPO (March); Furry Scurry, Denver Dumb Friends League Benefit (May); Littleton Historical Museum; National Western Stock Show and Rodeo (January); Rocky Mountain Pet EXPO (November)

DANIELS PARK WILDLIFE PRESERVE

There are over 1,000 acres of land in this Park. Most of it is a preserve for 50 buffalo who are kept within a large fenced-in area, and for many other kinds of wildlife who run free. The big, brawny buffalo, with their shaggy hair, curved horns, and humped back, may be seen from the road that cuts through the Park and borders their grazing land. If you're very quiet and a good detective, you may see some elk, antelope, deer, wild turkey, coyote, and perhaps a colony of prairie dogs. Keep alert and use your binoculars to hunt them down. How many do you think you'll see? Good luck, detectives!

Where is it? On Daniels Park Road in Sedalia, around 20 miles south of Denver. Take Route I-25 south to either Lincoln Avenue or Castle Pines Exits. Drive south approximately three miles to the Park.
Phone number? 660-9853.
Parking? Yes, and it's <u>free</u>.
Other transportation? No.
Open what days and hours? Daily from 5:00 a.m. to 11:00 p.m.

Entrance Fees? None. It's <u>free</u>.
View points? The road that cuts through the Park borders the buffalo grazing area. Don't miss the magnificent view overlooking the plains and the mountains.
Wheelchair accessible? Partially.
Food? No.
Restrooms? Yes, the out-house variety.

Related places of interest: *Denver Museum of Natural History; Denver Zoo; Genesee Park Buffalo and Elk Ranch; Lookout Mountain Nature Center; National Center for Atmospheric Research; Rocky Mountain Arsenal National Wildlife Refuge*

GENESEE PARK BUFFALO AND ELK RANCH

Buffalo and elk are awesome animals! Many years ago there were thousands of them roaming around Colorado. What a sight that must have been! There are only 40 buffalo in this herd.

The 41 elk stand tall and trim. Their antlers look like large tree branches. While you're looking, try listening. Can you hear the sounds buffalo and elk make? Try sniffing, too. How do they smell?

When you're through looking for buffalo and elk, you might want to go to Genesee Park and take a hike, run about, catch a ball or a frisbee, or capture a butterfly, and maybe even have a picnic.

Where is it? About 20 miles west of Denver in Golden. Drive on Route I-70 and take Exit 254. Watch for the sign, "Buffalo Herd Overlook" just before the exit.
Phone number? 526-1550.

Parking? Yes, and it's <u>free</u>.
Other transportation? RTD buses stop nearby.
Entrance Fees? None. It's <u>free</u>.
Viewing points? The animals graze in three pastures. Follow the signs leading to the Buffalo Herd Overlook. If you don't see them there, drive on I-70 to the Chief Hosa Exit, #253. Turn off the ramp to the Chief Hosa Campground and Lodge. Then take the dirt road to the left and follow it down to the buffalo and elk enclosures and the ranger's house. If the animals aren't there, go back across the bridge where you exited I-70, and take a very sharp right turn on the dirt and gravel road. Continue to the first turn-off. The animals may be grazing here. Good luck!
Wheelchair accessible? Partially.
Food? No.
Restrooms? Yes, at Genesee Park, nearby.

Related places of interest: Daniels Park Wildlife Preserve; Denver Museum of Natural History; Denver Zoo; Lookout Mountain Nature Center; National Center for Atmospheric Research; National Western Stock Show and Rodeo (January); Rocky Mountain Arsenal National Wildlife Refuge

HAWKQUEST'S CLASSROOM IN THE WILD

Have you ever seen hawks or eagles close-up and then seen them in free-flight over the prairie? Would you like to watch hawks hunt together and see the animals they chase try to escape? All these real-life, on-the-spot experiences are open to you in HawkQuest's Classroom in the Wild. This is truly awesome!

Where is it? The Classroom is held in one of three open fields in Aurora. Call for information.
Phone number? 690-6959.
Parking? Yes, and it's <u>free</u>.
Other transportation? No.
Open when? From September through May, but visits must be scheduled and paid for in advance.
Program? A two-hour program which takes place out on the prairie in Aurora. When you call to arrange your visit, you will be informed in which field and at what time the Classroom will meet. You will observe free-flying Harris hawks hunt wild game, and see the hawks working together to catch their prey while the small animals they pursue attempt to elude them. After the hawks have flown, HawkQuest's Golden eagle is released in free flight.
Program fees? Children, $10.00; adults, $15.00.
Wheelchair accessible? No.
Food? No.
Restrooms? No.

Related places of interest: Bald Eagle Days (January); Denver Museum of Natural History; Denver Zoo; HawkWatch and Count; Rocky Mountain Arsenal National Wildlife Refuge

Bald Eagle in flight.
Photo: Rocky Mountain Arsenal National Wildlife Refuge by
Wendy Shattil & Rob Rozinski

HAWKWATCH AND COUNT

Would you like to be a scientist for a day? Join the scientists at HawkWatch in April, when they Count the hawks as they fly over the lookout point. You may see as many as 17 different types of hawks, though most of them are red-tails. Bring your binoculars, a bottle of water, and sun screen.

Where is it? At the HawkWatch site on top of the Dakota Hogback, near the geological cross-section on Interstate 70 at the Morrison interchange exit.
Phone number? Colorado Bird Observatory, 659-4348.
Program? Count migrating hawks as they pass overhead. HawkWatch calls for volunteers of all ages to help.
Parking? Yes, and it's <u>free</u>.
Other transportation? RTD buses stop nearby.
Open what days and hours? Call 659-4348 for this information.
Entrance Fees? None. It's <u>free</u>. It is a cooperative project of the Colorado Bird Observatory and the Denver Museum of Natural History and they welcome volunteers.
Wheelchair accessible? No.
Food? No.
Restrooms? No.

Related places of interest: Bald Eagle Days (January); Denver Museum of Natural History; Rocky Mountain Arsenal National Wildlife Refuge

LOOKOUT MOUNTAIN NATURE CENTER: WILDLIFE PRESERVE

Stop! Look! Listen! Keep your eyes open! Do you see any bent twigs, foot prints, animal scat? Keep your ear cocked. Do you hear any grunts, growls, or grumbles? Keep your nose in the air. Do you sniff any animals nearby? There are 110 acres to explore in this Wildlife Preserve, where animals are kept safe and you can watch them going about their daily lives. Bring along your binoculars as well as trail food and water, and have fun animal tracking.

Where is it? At 910 Colorow Road in Golden, at the top of Lookout Mountain. Drive west on Route I-70 and take Exit 256. It's a five-minute drive from there. Follow the brown and white signs to the Jefferson County Conference and Nature Center.

Phone numbers? 526-0594; hearing impaired, 271-5026.

Parking? Yes, and it's <u>free</u>.

Open what days and hours? Trails are open daily, 8:00 a.m. to dusk. The Center is open Tuesdays through Sundays, 10:00 a.m. to 4:00 p.m.

Entrance fee? None. It's <u>free</u>.

Wheelchair accessible? Yes, but the trails exceed maximum grade.

Food? No.

Restrooms? Yes, in the Nature Center building; open between 10:00 a.m. and 4:00 p.m.

Related places of interest: Daniels Park Wildlife Preserve; Denver Museum of Natural History Wildlife Exhibit; Genesee Park; National Center for Atmospheric Research: Nature Preserve; National Trail Days (June); Rocky Mountain Arsenal National Wildlife Refuge

NATIONAL CENTER FOR ATMOSPHERIC RESEARCH (NCAR): NATURE PRESERVE

When a place is called a Nature Preserve, that means it is a safe place for the animals, flowers, shrubs, and trees. And it's where people like you and me can get close up to the deer. They're friendly and they expect that you will be, too. And, if you're an especially sharp trail-detective, you may see their footprints where they crossed the hiking trails. Look for some other critters walking or crawling along...two-legged, four-legged, six-legged, and maybe even one-hundred legged! You can try calling out their names if you have a picture book of insects with you. Maybe they'll stop and say hello.

Bring along your binoculars and a magnifying glass, too, to make the far-away and close-up creatures look even bigger. And don't forget a trail snack and plenty of water to keep from getting too tired and fussy. Have a great time!

Where is it? At West Table Mesa Drive in Boulder. Drive south on Broadway to South Boulder Road, turn right and continue out to where it becomes Table Mesa Drive. Stay on Table Mesa Drive to the NCAR parking lot. Inside the lobby, at the kiosk, you will find information about the trails.

Phone number? 441-3950.

Parking? Yes, and it's <u>free</u>.

Other transportation? RTD buses stop nearby but run infrequently. Call 443-0100 for times.

Open what days and hours? Everyday, dawn to dusk.

Entrance Fees? None. It's <u>free</u>.

Wheelchair accessible? Partially; the Walter Orr Roberts Mesa Nature Trail and NCAR's building.

Food? Yes, in the NCAR cafeteria, weekdays, 8:00 a.m. to 5:00 p.m.

Restrooms? Yes, off the NCAR lobby, weekdays, 8:00 a.m. to 5:00 p.m.

Related places of interest: *Bald Eagle Days (January); Daniels Park Wildlife Preserve; Denver Museum of Natural History Wildlife Exhibit; Lookout Mountain Nature Center: Wildlife Preserve; Rocky Mountain Arsenal National Wildlife Refuge*

Mule deer.
Photo: National Center for Atmospheric Research/UCAR/NSF

ROCKY MOUNTAIN ARSENAL
NATIONAL WILDLIFE REFUGE

Oh, deer! I don't want to bug you, but this place should be at the top of your list of places to visit. The Refuge is teeming with wildlife day and night, and they're not in cages. There are animals, birds, and insects galore in the three types of habitats the Refuge supports: the prairie, the wetlands, and the woodlands. For example, raptors, such as owls, hawks, and eagles, live on the prairie along with the prairie dogs, pocket gophers, kangaroo rats, and mice. In the wetlands, there are cranes, great blue herons, Canada geese, ducks, kingfishers, coots, bitterns, pelicans, rails, and grebes, along with beaver, salamanders, frogs, toads, and snakes. Living among the trees in the woodlands are lark buntings, meadowlarks, swallows, blue birds, western tanagers, and warblers, in addition to the badgers, racoons, wolves, coyotes, mule deer, and white-tailed deer. All three habitats support a great many insects, such as bees, mosquitos, flies, caterpillars, moths, and butterflies. And you can join the Rangers in restoring the land by planting native grasses and wildflowers and by learning about protecting the environment and actually doing it. This place is a paradise for wildlife, and for you too!

Where is it? Ten miles from downtown Denver, in Commerce City on what had been the Rocky Mountain Arsenal, 27 square miles of open land which is a Superfund clean-up site. As the clean up progresses, portions of the site are incorporated into the Refuge for environmental education and for viewing wildlife. It is managed by the U.S. Fish and Wildlife Service. Drive east on Route I-70 to Quebec Street and continue north on Quebec Street to 72nd Avenue where you'll see the entrance to the Arsenal on your left. Wait in the parking lot by the entrance to be picked up by a park service vehicle.

Phone number? Information and registration, 289-0232. You must call in advance of visiting.

Parking? Yes, and it's <u>free</u>.

Other transportation? RTD buses stop nearby; call RTD for times.

Open what days and hours? Until the remaining Arsenal land has been cleaned up of toxic chemical waste, the Wildlife Refuge will be opened on a very limited basis. Quarterly schedules of activities offered are mailed out to anyone requesting one by phone.

Fox cubs at play.
Photo: Rocky Mountain Arsenal National Wildlife Refuge &
Wendy Shattil & Rob Rozinski

Programs? Most programs are scheduled on weekends. Some of those offered in the past included wildlife bus tours on a Friday night, and on Saturday mornings and afternoons. There also are Special Events Days, such as a Halloween, endangered species costume contest and party, Bald Eagle Days, wild flower walks, participation in deer counts, and a special family catch-and-release fishing day.
Entrance Fees? None. It's _free_, but registration is required. Call in advance.
Wheelchair accessible? Partially.
Food? No.
Restrooms? Yes.

Related activities of interest: Bald Eagle Days (January); Chatfield Arboretum; Daniels Park Wildlife Preserve; Denver Botanic Gardens; Denver Museum of Natural History Wildlife Exhibit; Lookout Mountain Nature Center: Wildlife Preserve; National Center for Atmospheric Research: Nature Preserve; National Trail Days (June)

SETTLERS PARK AND
BOULDER CREEK PATH BIRD WALKS

Some people say Settlers Park is "for the birds" and that Boulder creaks. You can check these out on Saturday morning bird walks with a guide from the Wild Bird Center. Bring your binoculars and a hat.

Where is it? At the west end of Pearl Street in the Settlers Park parking lot.
Phone number? 442-1322, the Wild Bird Center Shop.
Parking? Yes, and it's _free_.

Other transportation? RTD buses and HOP shuttles stop nearby.

Open what days and hours? Saturdays, year-round. Meet in the parking lot of the Park at 7:50 a.m.

Fees? No, they are <u>free</u>.

Wheelchair accessible? Mostly.

Restrooms? No.

Related places of interest: Bald Eagle Days (January); Barr Lake State Park Bird Banding; Cherry Creek, Highline Canal, and Platte River Greenways; HawkQuest; HawkWatch and Count; National Center for Atmospheric Research: Nature Preserve

TROUT WATCHING

Would you like to stare a trout in the eye and still keep dry? There are two places right in Boulder to visit on a sunny day in summer or winter. It's fun to watch them breathe underwater, too. Do you know how they do it? Find out and tell a friend.

Where are they? Through the port holes of the Boulder Creek retaining wall in back of Clarion Harvest House at 1345 28th Street in Boulder, and in the 414 gallon trout aquarium near the main entrance and the children's areas of Boulder's Main Public Library at 1000 Canyon Road.

Phone number? Boulder Main Public Library, 441-3100.

Parking? Yes, and it's <u>free</u>.

Open what days and hours? Daylight hours for the Boulder Creek location, weather permitting; for library hours, call 441-3099.

Entrance Fees? None. It's <u>free</u>.

Related places of interest: *Bear Creek Lake Park; Boulder Reservoir; Cherry Creek State Park; Evergreen Lake Park; Rocky Mountain Arsenal National Wildlife Refuge; Utah Park; Washington Park*

ANIMALS FROM AROUND THE WORLD

THE DENVER ZOO

It's an Alphabet Zoo! See if you can find an Anteater, Bear, Camel, Deer, Elephant, Fox, Gorilla, Hippopotamus, Ibis, Jackal, Kangaroo, Leopard, Monkey, Napier, Ostrich, Puma, Quail, Rhinoceros, Snake, Turtle, Ungulate, Vulture, Walrus, Xenopus, Yak, and Zebra. Can you come up with your own Alphabet Zoo?

Where is it? At East 23rd Avenue and Steele Street in City Park, Denver. Drive east on 17th Avenue to Steele Street. Turn left and continue to 23rd Avenue. Turn right to enter the park.

Phone numbers? General: 331-4100; hearing impaired: 370-8093.

Parking? Yes, and it's <u>free</u>.

Other transportation? RTD buses and the Cultural Connection Trolley stop nearby.

Open what days and hours? Summer: everyday, 9:00 a.m. to 6:00 p.m.; winter: everyday, 10:00 a.m. to 5:00 p.m.

Entrance fees? Children under 3 years old, <u>free</u>; 4 to 12 year olds and senior adults 62 and older, $3.00; other adults, $4.00. Admission is <u>free</u> on Mondays for everyone.

Special events? See list in Chapter 6, *Looking Ahead: Adventures by the Month*, under June, October, and December.
Wheelchair accessible? Yes.
Food? Yes.
Restrooms? Yes.

Getting Around the Zoo
Zooliner? An open air vehicle that travels the zoo paths at regular intervals, spring through fall. Children under 3 years old, free; children over 3 and senior adults, $1.00; other adults, $1.50.
Stroller rental? $1.50 per day, at the entry gate.
Wagon rental? $2.50 per day, at the entry gate.
Wheelchair rental? $1.50 per day, at the gift shop.

Exhibits
African and Indian Wildlife: Includes lions, tigers, elephants, zebras, rhinoceroses, hippopotami, camels, and giraffes.
Birds from Around the World: Includes egrets, pelicans, peacocks, geese, and ducks.
North and South American Wildlife: Includes polar bears, black bears, mountain sheep, sea lions, penguins, and llamas.
Primates from Around the World: Includes many varieties within each grouping of primates. The new and expanded Primate House is due to open in the spring of 1996.
Tropical Discovery: Includes tropical plants, snakes, fish, newts, frogs, and crocodiles.

Animal Feeding Times
Penguins: 10:15 a.m. and 4:00 p.m.

Sea Lions: 11:00 a.m. and 2:30 p.m.
Primates at the Primate House: 3:00 p.m.
Felines at the Feline House: 3:30 p.m., except Mondays, a fast day.

Miniature Train Ride
Due to open in the spring of 1995, near the elephant exhibit. There will be a small cost per ride.

Related places of interest: *Bald Eagle Days (January); Boo at the Zoo (October); Conservation Day at the Zoo (June); Daniels Park Wildlife Preserve; Denver Museum of Natural History; Genesee Park Buffalo and Elk Ranch; National Center for Atmospheric Research; National Western Stock Show and Rodeo (January); Ringling Brothers and Barnum and Bailey Circus (October); Rocky Mountain Arsenal National Wildlife Refuge; Run for the Zoo (October); Shrine Three-ring Circus (March and April); Wildlights at the Denver Zoo (December)*

Poison Dart Frog.

Photo: Denver Zoo

Caitlin Rucker enjoying the Collage Energize! exhibit.
Photo: Sharon Carney Solomon

CHAPTER 4

Exploring Worlds:
Indoor and Outdoor Museums

What is the first thing you think of when you hear the word, "museum"? Do you think of a big building, with pictures hanging on the walls, with stuffed animals behind glass, or with lots of things to see and not to touch? If you do, you're partly right. That's one kind of museum, but even this kind of museum may have things for you to touch, like the Denver Museum of Natural History. There are other kinds of museums as well. There are some that have indoor and outdoor exhibits, like the Littleton Historic Museum and Denver Botanic Gardens. And there are others that have

Colorado Diorama.
Photo: Denver Museum of Natural History

their primary exhibits outdoors, such as Dinosaur Ridge and the Dakota Hogback, and they aren't called museums at all. Some museums show-and-tell about what it was like in the olden days. Others help you learn about rocks, weather, planets, and extinct and endangered animals. There are those that inform you about how money, tea, and newspapers are produced, and how airports work. Several museums will teach you how to make things and show you the things that other people have made. There are so many different museums to go to, from those displaying toys and dolls, to those showing cars, fire-engines, planes, and a space station, and they are all described below.

INDOOR MUSEUMS

ARVADA HISTORY MUSEUM
AND ART GALLERY

Learning the stories about the Plains Indians and the first pioneers who came to Arvada can be fun by sniffing, touching, looking, listening, and making believe you were one of them. Does this sound like fun or what? And after you finish poking around the History Museum, you might want to stop by at the Art Gallery to see their latest exhibit. The last I heard, it was about bikes, kites, and puppets from around the world. How does that grab you?

Where is it? At the Arvada Center for the Arts and Humanities, 6901 Wadsworth Boulevard in Arvada. Drive out Route I-70 to the South Wadsworth Boulevard Exit. At the end of the ramp, turn south to the Center.
Phone number? 431-3080, Extension 3460.

Parking? Yes, and it's <u>free</u>.
Other transportation? RTD buses stop nearby.
Open what days and hours? Mondays through Saturdays, 9:00 a.m. to 5:00 p.m.; Sundays, 1:00 to 5:00 p.m.
Entrance fees? None. It's <u>free</u>.
Exhibits? The Museum is actually an original 1864 log cabin, the Haines log house, that was found at Blunn Reservoir, disassembled and reassembled in the Arvada Center for the Arts and Humanities. Interactive exhibits tell about Arvada's early settlers, using all of your senses. The Arvada Center schedules participation plays for children in the Museum. Call 431-3964 for reservations and information.
Tours? Free docent-led tours of the exhibits by appointment only, otherwise they are self-guiding. Call 429-8157.
Wheelchair accessible? Yes.
Food? No.
Restrooms? Yes.

Related places of interest: *Aurora History Museum; Belmar Museum and Historic Village; Black American West Museum and Heritage Center; Boulder History Museum; Colorado History Museum; D.A.R. Pioneer Museum; Denver History Museum and the Evans-Byers House; Denver Museum of Miniatures, Dolls, and Toys; Four-Mile Historic Park; Hiwan Homestead House; Littleton Historic Museum; Molly Brown House*

AURORA HISTORY MUSEUM

Step into Aurora's Attic and you'll see what life was like up to 100 years ago. Be a history detective and find out if they had large shopping malls, brick houses, movies, paved roads, traffic lights, cars, and trucks. And find out what they had in the old days that you don't have today. Use your eyes, ears, and nose to sniff out the facts, and have fun doing it!

Where is it? In a red brick building at 15001 East Alameda Street, across from the Aurora Mall. Drive east on Alameda until you reach the Mall.
Phone number? 340-2220
Parking? Yes, and it's free. The parking lot is shared by the adjoining library.
Other transportation? RTD buses stop nearby.
Open what days and hours? Tuesdays through Sundays, 11:00 a.m. to 4:00 p.m.; closed on Mondays.
Entrance fees? Children $1.00; all others, $2.00; Sunday's free.
Exhibits? Aurora's Attic is a permanent exhibit depicting 100 years of Aurora's history. There are a few hands-on activities and a children's section will be ready by 1995. Special exhibits have included Contemporary Black Artists, and Funerary Temples and Mummification in Ancient Egypt.
Tours? Self-guided, only.
Wheelchair accessible? Yes.
Food? No.
Restrooms? Yes.

Related places of interest: Arvada History Museum and Art Gallery; Belmar Museum and Historic Village; Black American West Museum and Heritage Center; Boulder

History Museum; Colorado History Museum; D.A.R. Pioneer Museum; Denver History Museum and the Evans-Byers House; Denver Museum of Miniatures, Dolls, and Toys; Four-Mile Historic Park; Hiwan Homestead House; Littleton Historic Museum; Molly Brown House

BLACK AMERICAN WEST MUSEUM AND HERITAGE CENTER

Did you know that one third of all the cowboys in the west were African-Americans? And did you know that there were other Black settlers here in Colorado besides cowboys? Some were farmers, scouts, and miners. This Museum tells you what you ought to know about these people and their families and shows you what life was like for them on the American frontier.

The Cowboy Room.
Photo: Black American West Museum and
Heritage Center

Where is it? At 3091 California Street in downtown, north Denver.

Phone number? 292-2566.

Parking? Yes, and it's <u>free</u>.

Other transportation? Light Rail and RTD buses stop nearby.

Open what days and hours? Wednesdays through Fridays, 10:00 a.m. to 2:00 p.m.; Saturdays, 12:00 a.m. to 5:00 p.m.; Sundays, 2:00 to 5:00 p.m.; closed Mondays and Tuesdays.

Exhibits? Tell about the roles of Black people in Colorado from the early 1800s, after the Civil War, and up through the early 1920s. Permanent exhibits include a Homestead Room, Cowboy Room, and Miner Room. One of the special exhibits in 1994 was about Buffalo Soldiers.

Entrance fees? Children 12 and under, 50 cents; youth 12 to 17, 75 cents; senior adults, $1.50; other adults, $2.00.

Wheelchair accessible? Partially.

Food? No.

Restrooms? Yes.

Related places of interest: African Arts Family Day (October); Buffalo Bill's Memorial Museum and Grave; Colorado History Museum; Colorado Performing Arts Festival (September); D.A.R. Pioneer Museum; Denver Art Museum African Art Exhibit; Denver Black Arts Festival (July); Denver History Museum and the Byers-Evans House; Denver Museum of Miniatures, Dolls, and Toys; Eulipions Cultural Center; Hiwan Homestead House; Hue-Man Experience Bookstore; Juneteenth Annual Celebration (June); Kwansaa Celebration (December); Mizel Museum of Judaica; Molly Brown House; National Western Stock Show and Rodeo (January)

BOULDER DAILY CAMERA

What's black and white and read all over? You're right if you said a newspaper. Isn't it amazing that every day there's a newspaper with the latest news stories? If you would like to see how a newspaper is made, you can visit the Boulder Daily Camera offices and see it happen right before your eyes. Awesome!

Where is it? 1048 Pearl Street in Boulder. Drive north on 28th Street to Pearl Street. Turn left and continue on Pearl Street to 10th Street.

Phone number? 473-1508.

Parking? Yes, and it's <u>free</u> in the front lot; request a token on the way out to use when leaving the lot.

Other transportation? RTD buses and the HOP shuttles stop nearby.

Open what days and hours? Mondays through Fridays; call Betsy Abbott for an appointment.

Entrance fees? None. It's <u>free</u>.

Tour? A very comprehensive guided tour through the entire process of news gathering, newspaper composing, and news printing. Includes visits to the camera room, press room, mail room, composing room, news room, and classified and retail department.

Wheelchair accessible? Yes.

Food? Yes.

Restroom? Yes.

Related places of interest: Celestial Seasonings Tea Company; United States Mint

BOULDER MUSEUM OF HISTORY

Did you ever wonder what it was like living in Boulder a long time ago? Well, here's your chance to learn about life in Boulder in the old days. Compare your dentist's and doctor's offices with the old ones at the Museum. Look at the dolls and toys. How are they different from yours...besides being a lot older? Try on some old-fashioned clothes. Do they make you feel strangely different? They may help you to make believe you are a different person after all.

Where is it? At 1206 Euclid Avenue in Boulder. Driving north on Broadway, turn right on 16th Street and right again on Euclid Avenue. The Museum is between 12th and 13th Streets.
Phone number? 449-3464.
Parking? Yes, and it's free and located on the east side of the Museum.
Other transportation? RTD buses and the HOP shuttles stop nearby.
Open what days and hours? Tuesdays to Saturdays, 12:00 to 4:00 p.m.
Entrance fees? Children under 12 are free; 12 year-olds and adults, $1.00.
Exhibits? The Museum is an 1899 landmark which accommodates seven exhibits devoted to Boulder's history of mining, ranching, and farming; artifacts and photographs of everyday life; a 1920s kitchen and period drawing room; a "medicine" room of dentist, pharmacist, and physician's furniture and equipment; and a room with homemade quilts, coverlets, vintage clothing, a two-story doll house, dolls, toys, and games. There are clothes children can try on but no other interactive exhibits.

Tour? Self-guided only.
Wheelchair accessible? Partially.
Food? No.
Restroom? Yes.

Related places of interest: Aurora History Museum; Arvada History Museum and Art Gallery; Belmar Museum and Historical Village; Colorado History Museum; D.A.R. Pioneer Museum; Denver History Museum and the Byers-Evans House; Denver Museum of Miniatures, Dolls, and Toys; Four-Mile Historic Park; Hiwan Homestead House; Littleton Historical Museum; Molly Brown House

CELESTIAL SEASONINGS TEA COMPANY

Did you know that "herb" is not only the short name for Herbert, it's also a plant that can be used to flavor food and to make into tea. In fact, there are many herbs that are grown in and around Boulder, and elsewhere, that are made into tea at the Celestial Seasonings Tea Company. If you suffer from curiosi-tea, you'll enjoy seeing how it is produced from start to finish.

Where is it? At 4600 Sleepytime Drive in Boulder. Drive north on Foothills Parkway (Route 157) to Jay Road and turn right. Continue to Spine Road and turn left. The Tea Company is ¾ of-a-mile down Spine Road, on the left side.
Phone number? 581-1202, tour information.
Parking? Yes, and it's <u>free</u>.
Other transportation? RTD buses stop nearby.
Open what days and hours? Mondays through Saturdays, 10:00 a.m. to 3:00 p.m.; closed on major holidays.

Entrance fees? None. It's <u>free</u>.
Tour? A guided tour starts every hour from 10:00 a.m. to closing and takes you through the whole plant. You learn about the history of the company, experience tea-tasting, walk by the offices and see the entire tea production line from milling to mixing to packaging to shipping. For children over 5 years old only.
Wheelchair accessible? Yes.
Food? Yes.
Restrooms? Yes.

Related places of interest: Boulder Daily Camera; Chatfield Arboretum; Denver Botanic Gardens; United States Mint

CHAMBERLIN OBSERVATORY

Did you ever look up at the sky at night and wonder about all the twinkling points of light? Would you like to know what they are? how they got there? where they're going? Are you curious about meteors, satellites, planets, the moon, the earth, and the stars? Chamberlin Observatory is a place to find out some of the answers from their summer and winter sky programs.

Where is it? At Observatory Park, 2930 East Warren Avenue in Denver. Drive south on Broadway to Evans Avenue and turn left. Continue on Evans Avenue, past University Avenue to East Warren Avenue and turn right. Continue on Warren to the Observatory.
Phone numbers? 871-2238 and 871-3222.
Parking? <u>Free</u>, on-the-street parking.

Other transportation? RTD buses stop nearby.

Open what days and hours? Summer Skies: Tuesdays and Thursdays, 8:30 to 10:00 p.m.; Winter Skies: alternate Tuesdays and Thursdays, 7:00 to 9:30 p.m.

Programs? Summer Skies and Winter Skies programs are sponsored by the University of Denver and the Denver Astronomical Society. They include slide shows, lectures, and, weather permitting, telescope viewing of the skies. Reservations are required.

Entrance fees? Children 13 years old and younger, $1.00; adults, $2.00.

Wheelchair accessible? Yes.

Food? No.

Restrooms? Yes.

Related places of interest: Charles C. Gates Planetarium; Christmas at Fiske (December); Fiske Planetarium; Wings Over the Rockies Aviation and Space Museum

CHARLES C. GATES PLANETARIUM

Did you ever look through a real telescope and see a planet, or a meteor, or a satellite? If its a clear night on the first Tuesday of any month, go to the Charles C. Gates Planetarium and you'll get a look at our Denver sky through a telescope. That's not all. There are some great shows at the Planetarium, too, like the ones called *Star Trek* and *The Little Star that Could.*

Where is it? On the 1st floor of the Denver Museum of Natural History in City Park at 2001 Colorado Boulevard in Denver. Drive east on 17th Avenue to Colorado Boulevard.

Turn left and turn left again at 20th Street, at the museum entrance.

Phone numbers? Members, 322-7009; nonmembers, 370-6351; and hearing impaired, 370-8257.

Parking? Yes, and it's free.

Other transportation? RTD buses and the Cultural Connection Trolley stop nearby.

Strollers? Rent for $1.00.

Open what days and hours? Year-round, everyday, 12:30, 1:30, and 2:30 p.m. On weekends, an additional show-time is at 3:30 p.m.

Programs? Multi-media and laser shows are presented in a simulated, star-system environment. On the first Tuesday of every month, at 6:00 p.m., see *Colorado Skies*, a live presentation of what's going on in our sky. Weather and time permitting, telescopes may be set up for live viewing of the night sky following the show. Reserve tickets by calling 322-7009.

Special programs in the 1994-95 season included the following: *Bugs; To Worlds Beyond; Orion Rendezvous: A Star Trek Voyage of Discovery;* and *The Little Star That Could.* Call for current programs, dates, and times, and reservations.

Entrance fees? Members: children 4 to 12 years old, $1.25; adults, $1.75. Nonmembers: children and senior adults, $2.50; other adults, $3.50. Ask about buying a combined ticket with IMAX Theater to get a better price.

Wheelchairs? Yes, and they're free.

Wheelchair accessible? Yes.

Food? Yes.

Restrooms? Yes.

Related places of interest: Chamberlin Observatory; Christmas at Fiske (December); Fiske Planetarium; Wings Over the Rockies Aviation and Space Museum

CHILDREN'S MUSEUM

Would you like to make believe you're a cartoon artist, a teller in a bank, a cashier in a super-market, a skier on a big mountain, and a scientist at work in your laboratory? You can do all of these things, and more, at the Children's Museum. You can try moving around in a wheelchair or show-off what you can do if you're already using one. And you can make your own "totem". This is a great place to explore and to discover.

Where is it? At 2121 Children's Museum Drive in Denver. Take Route I-25 to Exit 211 (23rd Avenue) and go east to 7th Street; turn right and right again on Children's Museum Drive.
Phone number? 433-7444.
Parking? Yes, and it's <u>free</u>.
Other transportation? RTD buses, the Cultural Connection Trolley, and the Platte Valley Trolley stop nearby.
Open what days and hours? Winter: Tuesdays through Saturdays, 10:00 a.m. to 5:00 p.m.; Sundays, noon to 5:00 p.m.; closed Mondays. Summer: everyday, 10:00 a.m. to 5:00 p.m., starting early in June. There is a Toddler Hour every Tuesday, from 9:00 to 10:00 a.m., year-round.
Entrance fees? Friday nights, 5:30 to 8:00 p.m., <u>free</u>; members and children under 2 years old, <u>free</u>; adults and children 2 to 60 years old, $4.00; over 60, $1.50.
Special events? Look in Chapter 6, Adventures by the Month, under April, October, and December.
Wheelchair accessible? Yes.
Food? Yes, at Dr. Dabble's Drive-In Cafe (see description below).
Restrooms? Yes.
Birthday parties? Yes.

Exhibits

Bank On It!: Hands-on activities that focus on money, it's value by weight and purchasing power, the cycle of earning, saving, and spending, and the bank environment with computer stations and a vault.

DiscoveryLABS: Experiments are encouraged in three LABS. The *EarthLAB* has water-and wind-erosion tables for exploration, and a News 4 weather studio with a Chromokey Wall, where information can be gathered and reported. The *ScienceLAB* has sound, light, and hydroponics rooms, an electricity area, and various equipment to manipulate, such as pendulums and puzzles. The *ComputerLAB* has 20 computers with programs ranging from very simple to fairly complex.

Dr. Dabble's Drive-In Cafe: This center combines the restaurant area with hands-on opportunities for learning about early animation techniques and for providing the sound effects for a cartoon.

KidSlope: Ski lessons are given here year-round. See the write up in Chapter 2, *Keeping Fit*, under KidSlope at the Children's Museum.

King Soopers: A grocery store with baskets, packaged and canned food on shelves, and a check-out counter, creates a setting where roles of customer and cashier can be practiced.

Play Partners - The Three Bears House: A scaled-down cottage provides the play space to experience the *Three Bears* story and to explore contrasting concepts, such as hard and soft, hot and cold, and big and small.

Size Wise: Opportunity to compare your height, weight, arm span, and shoe size to life-size figures of some of the Denver Nuggets basketball players and their mascot, Rocky. There are two basketball nets at different heights to test your skills.

SpokesPeople: Features an indoor and outdoor environment that is suitable for children in wheelchairs. Opportunities are provided for exploring a variety of materials and activities in a wheelchair to increase your understanding about disability and safety.

Theater: Entertainment is scheduled on Friday nights and weekends. See description in Chapter 5, *Having More Fun,* under Theater, page 167.

Totems: Information on the totems of the North West Indians is presented along with a large magnetic board on which totems can be constructed.

Related places of interest: *Channel 4 Education EXPO (February); Colorado History Museum; Collage Children's Museum; Conservation Day at the Zoo (June); Denver Art Museum Native American Indian Exhibit; Denver Museum of Natural History Native American Indian Exhibit and Hall of Life Exhibit; Earth Day Celebrations at the Denver Museum of Natural History (April), at the Collage Children's Museum (April), and at Earthfest (April); National Center for Atmospheric Research; Noon-year's Eve (December); National Trail Days (June); Rocky Mountain River Festival (June); Trick or Treat Street (October); United States Mint*

COLLAGE CHILDREN'S MUSEUM

There are lots of ways to pretend at the Collage Museum. You can decide on what you want to be when you grow up by dressing up in the clothes worn by people who work at different jobs and you can pretend to be one of them. If you want to be a scientist, you can experiment with magnets and with paint, or you can create your own ball maze. But if you are more interested in looking like an animal, you can pull the wool over your eyes by dressing up like a sheep or some other fuzzy animal and pretend to be grazing out in the grassy fields. Whether you look like a person or an animal, its fun to see yourself in the mirrors that make you look different...tall and skinny, short and squat, or bent and curved in several places. After all this pretending, you might decide you'd rather be you...yourself...and nobody else.

Where is it? At 2065 30th Street, in Aspen Plaza, between Pearl and Walnut Streets in Boulder. Drive north on 28th Street to Pearl Street and turn right.
Phone number? 440-9894.
Parking? Yes, and it's <u>free</u>, on the street or at the Crossroads Mall.
Other transportation? RTD buses and HOP shuttles stop nearby.
Open what days and hours? Wednesdays, 2:00 to 5:00 p.m.; Thursdays to Saturdays, 10:00 a.m. to 5:00 p.m.; Sundays, 1:00 to 5:00 p.m.
Entrance fees? Museum members and children under two, <u>free</u>; all others, $2.00 or $7.00 per family. An adult must accompany children under 12.
Wheelchair accessible? Yes.

*Alan Soloman getting a hair-raising experience
at the Collage Energize! exhibit.*

Photo: Sharon Carney Soloman

Food? No.
Restrooms? Yes.
Birthday parties? Yes.

Exhibits
Image-ination: Consists of five exhibits on how we see and create pictures, such as pin screens, zoetrope, and a giant kaleidoscope.

Toddler's Playscape: An area in which to explore tactile experiences while developing gross-motor skills.

Ball Maze: Series of 3 foot by 3 foot slanting horizontal and vertical channels in which children create their own mazes with large and small balls.

Dress-up: Clothes to dress-up in, representing different work-roles and animals. Different kinds of lights and mirrors provide children with different ways of seeing themselves in the dress-up clothes.

Art Express: Explore art materials in creative ways, both structured and unstructured, such as learning about what happens when colors are mixed.

Marvelous Magnets: Explore the properties of magnets using steel filings.

Special Exhibits

Interactive Science Programs: Held every Saturday at 11:00 a.m. and 1:00 p.m., under the direction of Professor Laboratory.

Storytelling: The first Sunday of every month is devoted to the art of storytelling by a member of the Rocky Mountain Storyteller's Guild.

Sunday Stars: Music and theater performances from a variety of artists are presented the third Sunday of every winter month.

Annual Events: see Chapter 6, *Looking Ahead,* listings for February, April, October, and December.

Related places of interest: Channel 4 Education EXPO (March); Children's Museum; Chapter 5, music and theater listings; Conservation Day at the Zoo (June); Denver Art Museum Workshops; Denver Museum of Natural History Hall of Life Exhibit; Earth Day Celebrations at the Denver Museum of Natural History (April), at the Collage Children's Museum (April), and at Earthfest (April); El Dia De Los Muertes (October); Kwansaa Celebration (December); National Trail Days (June); Rocky Mountain River Festival (June)

COLORADO GOVERNOR'S MANSION

Have you ever been inside a mansion? Well, this is your chance. Each of the Governors of Colorado lived in this house during their time in office. Each Governor welcomes people to stop by on certain days of the year to see the beautiful furniture, lights, rugs, and art. This special house belongs to the people of Colorado who let the Governor and his family live there. If you're going to be the Governor some day, come and take a look at your future home.

Where is it? At 400 East 8th Avenue at Pennsylvania Street in Denver. Drive east on 6th Avenue and turn left on Pennsylvania Street.
Phone number? 866-3681.
Parking? On the street, where you find it and it's free.
Other transportation? RTD buses stop nearby.
Open what days and hours? May through August, Tuesdays only, 1:00 to 3:00 p.m.; Christmas tours one week in December; call for dates.
Entrance fees? No. It's free.
Exhibits? The Mansion contains art work from France, Italy, and China including French tapestries, 16th century carvings, and a Waterford chandelier from the 1800s that once hung in the White House.
Wheelchair accessible? Yes.
Food? No.
Restrooms? Yes.

Related places of interest: Colorado State Capitol; Colorado History Museum

COLORADO HISTORY MUSEUM

Say the word "history" in two parts, like "his-story." It could be his- or her- story, or the story about a whole group of people. When you go to the Colorado History Museum, you're going to find out about the story of Native Americans, Hispanic people, and other people who came to live in Colorado from all over the world. You'll find out about the buffalo hunters, cowboys, fur trappers, and miners. These stories are colorful and interesting, and they're told in many different ways, with dioramas, old photographs, slide and film shows, and with collections of things that were used in everyday life. You'll see a real covered wagon, tepee, and sod house, and some of the hand-tools and large machinery used by the miners to dig out gold and silver from the ground.

Where is it? At 1300 Broadway in downtown Denver across from the Main Public Library.
Phone number? 866-3681.
Parking? Parking is where you find it. Bring nickels, dimes, quarters, and dollar bills for parking meters or parking lot fees.
Other transportation? RTD buses and the Cultural Connection Trolley stop nearby.
Open what days and hours? Year-round, Mondays through Saturdays, 10:00 a.m. to 4:30 p.m.; Sundays, noon to 4:30 p.m.
Entrance fees? Children and senior adults, $1.50; other adults, $3.00.
Exhibits? There are both continuing and special exhibits that celebrate the diversity of the people who settled and live in Colorado, from the early 19th century to the present.

Which hat would you wear?
Photo: Colorado Historical Society

Some of these include: *Worlds Apart: Indians and Whites in Nineteenth Century Colorado; Out of the Earth: Mining in Colorado;* and *La Gente: Hispanos in Colorado.* In 1994-95, one special exhibit featured the history of Colorado's Black musicians, *Jazz.*
Wheelchair accessible? Yes.
Food? Yes.
Restrooms? Yes.

Related places of interest: Aurora History Museum; Arvada History Museum and Art Gallery; Belmar Museum *and Historic Village; Black American West Museum and Heritage Center; Boulder History Museum; Celebration of 1860s Work and Play (April); Colorado Indian Market and Western Art Roundup (January and July); D.A.R. Pioneer Museum; Denver History Museum and the Byers-Evans House; Denver Museum of Miniatures, Dolls, and Toys; Four-Mile Historic Park; Gold Panning in Clear Creek; Hiwan Homestead House; Littleton Historical Museum; Molly Brown House; Spirits of the Past (October)*

COLORADO RAILROAD MUSEUM

Did you know that in the old, old days, if you needed to travel long distances, you went by horseback or covered wagon? That was a very long time ago, even before we had trains. But when railroads were finally built, trains made long-distance travel much quicker and more comfortable.

There weren't any cars in those days, so for traveling short-distances in the cities, tracks were laid and trolleys ran on them, carrying people to offices, shops, and entertainment. I learned about this at the Colorado Railroad Museum, which tells you the story of trains and trolleys in the old, old days. You'll see steam engines, railroad cars, trolleys, and a model railroad.

Where is it? At 17155 West 44th Avenue in Golden. Travel west on 6th Avenue to the north Kipling Street exit. At 44th Avenue turn left and continue out another 5 miles.
Phone number? 279-4591.
Parking? Yes, and it's <u>free</u>.
Other transportation? RTD buses stop nearby weekdays only; no buses return to Denver between 3:00 and 4:00 p.m.

Open what days and hours? June through August, every-day, 9:00 a.m. to 6:00 p.m.; September through May, 9:00 a.m. to 5:00 p.m.
Entrance fees? Children 16 and under, $1.50; adults, $3.00; families, $6.50.
Wheelchair accessible? No.
Food? Yes.
Restrooms? Yes.

Related places of interest: Denver Auto Show; Denver Zoo Miniature Train Ride; Forney Transportation Museum; Lakeside Amusement Park Miniature Train Ride; Lion's Club Miniature Train Ride; Tiny Town Miniature Train Ride; Tri-State Auto Show (March); Union Pacific Railroad Station

COLORADO STATE CAPITOL

There are a lot of "Did you know" questions about our State Capitol. For example:

Did you know that Colorado's State Capitol was built to look like the United States Capitol in Washington, D.C.?

Did you know that the big round dome of Colorado's State Capitol is covered with real gold that was taken from Colorado mines?

Did you know that when you climb the steps on the west side of the State Capitol, you'll be exactly one mile above sea level?

Those are just a few of the fantastic facts that will amaze you when you take the free tour. See how many more "Did you knows... you can collect and tell your friends.

Where is it? At 200 Colfax Avenue in downtown Denver.

Phone number? 866-2604.

Parking? On the street, metered parking is where you can find it. Bring enough change.

Other transportation? RTD buses and the Cultural Connection Trolley stop nearby.

Open what days and hours? Weekdays only, from 9:00 a.m. to 3:00 p.m.

Entrance fees? None. All tours are <u>free</u>.

Tours? Mondays through Fridays, every hour, 9:30 a.m. to 2:30 p.m. You can go up to the dome 9:00 a.m. to 3:30 p.m. without taking the tour.

Wheelchair accessible? Yes.

Food? Yes, in the cafeteria which is open to the public, 7:00 a.m. to 3:30 p.m.

Restrooms? Yes.

Related places of interest: Colorado Governor's Mansion; Colorado History Museum

D.A.R. PIONEER MUSEUM

Did you ever wonder how Golden got its name and who decided on that name? There are lots of clues to get the answers in the many collections of things the early Golden settlers used in the old days. See if you can find the answers when you visit the Pioneer Museum.

Where is it? At 911 Tenth Street in Golden.

Phone number? 278-7151.

Parking? <u>Free</u> on-the-street parking.

Other transportation? RTD buses stop nearby.

Open what days and hours? Summer: Mondays through

Saturdays, 11:00 a.m. to 4:00 p.m. Winter: noon to 4:00 p.m. Closed Sundays and major holidays.

Entrance fees? None. It's <u>free</u>.

Exhibits? Primarily concerned with the history of Golden and its founders through exhibits of artifacts and portraits. There are displays of machinery related to gold mining, guns, clothing, and documents and other collections from the early 1700 and 1800s, as well as a collection of over 200 dolls made by various Native American tribes across the country.

Tours? Self-guided.

Wheelchair accessible? Yes.

Food? No.

Restrooms? Yes.

Related places of interest: Arvada History Museum and Art Gallery; Aurora History Museum; Belmar Historic Museum and Village; Black American West Museum and Heritage Center; Boulder History Museum; Colorado History Museum; Denver History Museum and the Byers-Evans House; Four-Mile Historic Park; Gold Panning in Clear Creek; Hiwan Homestead House; Littleton Historic Museum; Molly Brown House

DENVER ART MUSEUM

Do you remember the first time you ever drew with a crayon or painted a picture with a brush or with your fingers? Was it fun and do you still like to do it? Well, at the Denver Art Museum, you can see what people drew and painted who just couldn't stop doing it, studied it, and who became great at it. You can also see how a lot of people use art everyday in their lives, people who live in far-off places and people who live nearby. The great thing about this Museum is all the art projects you can do by coming to their workshops. This is one of the neatest, coolest, and "funnest" Museums to visit.

Where is it? At 14th Avenue and Bannock Street in downtown Denver.
Phone number? 640-2793.
Parking? Where you find it. Bring lots of change for meters or parking lots.
Other transportation? RTD buses and the Cultural Connection Trolley stop nearby.
Open what days and hours? Tuesdays through Saturdays, 10:00 a.m. to 5:00 p.m.; Sundays, noon to 5:00 p.m.; closed Mondays.
Entrance fees? Free admission Saturdays; children 6 and under free; 6-18 year-olds, students with an ID, and senior adults over 65 years old, $1.50; all others $3.00.
Wheelchairs? Yes, and they're free.
Wheelchair accessible? Yes.
Food? Yes.
Restrooms? Yes.

Workshops

Families Explore Materials: First and Third Saturdays, at 11:00 a.m., 12:30 p.m., and 2:00 p.m. Uses material in various projects which tend to be theme related, such as how New Mexican folk artists make images with straw. Then you make your own colorful straw inlay work. Call 640-5929 one week in advance for a place.

Family Backpacks: Second, fourth, and fifth Saturdays, 10:30 a.m. to 3:30 p.m. The backpacks contain hands-on games and activities that you use as you travel through the galleries. The trips include: Granny's Adventures in Africa; Spanish Colonial Splendors; Hindu Gods and Demons; Western Adventures; and Baskets, Pots, and Parfleches. Call 640-5929 for information.

Kids Corner: Each month, an activity is selected that relates to one of the exhibitions. For example, the children made Epa-style masks to honor heroes and ancestors and then they saw the Epa masks in the Exploring Africa exhibit. Another time, they colored and cut out finger puppets based on animal sculptures in the Asian art collection. Call 839-4811 for information.

Related places of interest: African Arts Family Day (October); Black American West Museum and Heritage Center; Boulder Creek Festival (May); Boulder History Museum; Channel 4 Education EXPO (March); Cherry Blossom Festival (May); Collage Children's Museum Birthday Celebration (February); Colorado History Museum; Colorado Indian Market and Western Art Roundup (January and July); Colorado Performing Arts Festival (September); Conservation day at the Zoo (June); Denver Black Arts Festival (July); Denver Museum of Miniatures, Dolls, and Toys; March Pow Wow (March); Old Fashioned Fourth of

July Family Picnic (July); Passport to Asia Festival (August); Two Free Days at the Denver Museum of Dolls, Toys, and Miniatures (August)

DENVER FIRE-FIGHTER'S MUSEUM

After a visit to your local fire station, come to the Denver Fire-Fighters Museum. Jump into fireman boots, put on a helmet, and climb up on the antique fire truck. You can pretend you're a fire-fighter in the early days of Denver's history. As you steer your engine down the street, clang the bell to warn the people to clear the way! And, if you're lucky, a guide will tell you all about the other equipment in the Museum, how to report a fire, and how to protect yourself from getting burned. Maybe this visit will help you to decide if you want to be a fire-fighter someday.

Where is it? At 1326 Tremont Place in Denver.
Phone number? 892-1436.
Parking? Parking is where you find it. Bring plenty of change for a parking lot or meter.
Other transportation? RTD buses stop nearby.
Open what days and hours? Year-round, Mondays through Fridays, 10:00 a.m. to 2:00 p.m.
Entrance fees? Children up to 12 years old, $1.00; all others, $2.00.
Wheelchair accessible? Yes.
Food? No.
Restrooms? Yes.
Birthday parties? Yes.

Related places of interest: *Colorado History Museum; Forest Fire-Fighter Center; Forney Transportation Museum*

DENVER HISTORY MUSEUM AND THE BYERS-EVANS HOUSE

Do you ever wonder what they mean when they talk about "the good old days"? Do you think things were better then than they are now? The Denver History Museum takes you back about 100 years so you can look at what the "good old days" were like for the Byers and Evans families who lived in the house where the Museum is located. You can look at all the things used by these families in their daily lives. There also are TV sets that will answer questions about how people lived in the old days just by pressing the screen. After a visit, perhaps you can decide which times look best to you, then or now.

Byers-Evans House.
Photo: Colorado Historical Society

Where is it? 1310 Bannock Street in downtown Denver.
Phone number? 620-4933
Parking? Metered parking on the street and in parking lots nearby. Bring change and dollar bills.
Other transportation? RTD buses and the Cultural Connection Trolley stop nearby.
Open what days and hours? Tuesdays through Sundays, 11:00 a.m. to 3:00 p.m.; closed Mondays.
Exhibits? The Museum is located in the Carriage House of the Byers-Evans House. The House was built in 1883 and restored to its early 20th century appearance. Two Denver pioneer families lived in the House at separate times. In addition to tours of the house, the Museum displays objects that were used and worn in Denver during the late 19th and early 20th centuries, and provides a great deal of information on Denver's history through interactive videos with touch screens.
Entrance fees? Children under six years old, free; 6 to 16 year-olds, $1.50; senior adults over 65, $2.50; other adults, $3.00; members of the Historical Society, free. One fee for the Museum and the Byers-Evans House.
Wheelchair accessible? Yes, if hand-and foot-rests can be collapsed on large chairs.
Food? No.
Restrooms? Yes.

Related places of interest: Arvada Museum; Aurora Museum; Boulder History Museum; Colorado History Museum; D.A.R. Pioneer Museum; Denver Fire-Fighter's Museum; Denver Museum of Miniatures, Dolls, and Toys; Four-Mile Historic Park; Hiwan Homestead House; Littleton Historic Museum; Molly Brown House

DENVER MUSEUM OF MINIATURES, DOLLS, AND TOYS

Black dolls, white dolls, big dolls, small dolls, furry dolls, smooth dolls, rag dolls and "cool dolls"...they'll stir up memories for children of all ages. You're likely to find your favorite doll here, whether it be Shirley Temple, Betsy Wetsy, Pooh-Bear, or any number of less well-known "lovables." Many were made by their owners. Plan your trip ahead of time and you may learn to make your own doll, too, and take it home with you. Don't forget to look at the doll houses with the teeny-tiny couches, chairs, rugs, pictures, dishes, stoves, bureaus, mirrors, sinks, toilets, curtains, pianos and all? Awesome!

If dolls and doll houses aren't your thing, how about toys your grandma and grandpa used to play with when they were your age? They look strange but interesting!

Where is it? At 1880 Gaylord Street in Denver.
Phone numbers? Information; 322-3704; reservations, 322-1053.
Parking? Yes, and it's <u>free</u> on-the-street parking.
Other transportation? RTD buses and the Cultural Connection Trolley stop nearby.
Open what days and hours? Year-round, Tuesdays through Saturdays, 10:00 a.m. to 4:00 p.m.; Sundays, 1:00 to 4:00 p.m.
Entrance fees? Children, $2.00; senior adults, $2.00; other adults, $3.00. There are two <u>free</u> weekends for Denver residents, during which there are art workshops, puppet shows, and storytelling. Call for dates.
Exhibits? Exhibits are changed twice a year and include very small dolls, toys, and pictures, as well as small and

large doll houses, and teddy bears. In addition, there are other activities scheduled throughout the year. There's lots to see in this small, historic Denver house, that looks a bit like a Victorian doll house, too.

Wheelchair accessible? No.
Food? No.
Restrooms? Yes.
Birthday parties? Yes.

Related places of interest: Belmar Museum and Historic Village; Boulder History Museum; Denver Art Museum; Denver Museum of Natural History; Littleton Historical Museum; Two Free Days at the Denver Museum of Miniatures, Dolls, and Toys (September)

Selection of toys from the Museum's collection.
Photo: Denver Museum of Miniatures, Dolls, and Toys

DENVER MUSEUM OF NATURAL HISTORY

Are you a dinofile? You are if you're nuts about the saurus family: the Allosaurus, Apatosaurus, Bracheosaurus, Campotosaurus, Stegosaurus, Tyrannosaurus, and Ultrasaurus...to name just a few. Well, don't miss going to the Denver Museum of Natural History if you are a dinofile where you'll see several of the above. For starters, you'll be greeted by a Tyrannosaurs Rex just beyond the front door and you'll be in dinosaur heaven in the new Prehistoric Journey exhibit that opens in October 1995. You'll walk through the land as it was billions of years ago, surrounded by ancient plants, mammals, and dinosaurs. And suddenly you'll be brought back to the present when you see todays scientists at work on real fossils, and take the time to play the special computer games designed especially for you.

There are lots of the other fabulous exhibits, too, at this Museum. You might even become a wild animal-o-file, a gem-o-file, an insect-o-file, or maybe even a Native American-o-file. There are several other "o-files" you might become by checking out some of the exhibits I haven't even mentioned yet. Take a look and see.

Where is it? At 2001 Colorado Boulevard in City Park, north east Denver.
Phone numbers? Members, 322-7009; non-members, 370-6351; hearing impaired, 370-8257.
Parking? Yes, and it's <u>free</u>.
Other transportation? RTD buses and the Cultural Connection Trolley stop near by.
Outside features? Facing west, see a grand view of the mountains and City Park lake, and two sculptures, one of a grizzly bear and another of a wolf pack. There also is a

Tyrannosaurs Rex skeleton.
Photo: Denver Museum of Natural History

grassy slope on this side of the museum which children enjoy rolling down between exhibits.
Strollers? Rent for $1.00.
Wheelchairs? Yes, and they're <u>free</u>.
Open what days and hours? Everyday, 9:00 a.m. to 5:00 p.m.; closed on Christmas day.
Entrance fees? Members, <u>free</u>; children $2.50; senior adults 65 years and older, $ 2.50; other adults, $4.50.
Wheelchair accessible? Yes.
Food? Yes.
Restrooms? Yes.

Exhibits
Entrance: Tyrannosaurs Rex skeleton.
First Floor: Butterflies, moths, and other insects; gems and minerals of the world; Mesa and South American Archaeology.
Second floor: Native North American Cultures; Hall of Life, which includes hands-on learning about the five senses, anatomy, fitness, nutrition, and drugs; Edge of the Wild: Colorado Wildlife Hall.
Third floor: Fossil Lab where you can watch scientists prepare plant and animal fossils; Prehistoric Journey, due to open in the fall of 1995; Explore Colorado, Botswana, and Africa.

Monthly Events
Treasure House: 3 to 5 year-olds explore a topic related to one of the Museum's collections by carrying out experimental activities and creative arts projects. It meets twice-a-week, seven sessions a month. Call 370-8276 for a brochure or 370-8287 for space availability.

Saturday and Summer Workshops
Science, Health, and Natural History Workshops: 3 to 12 year-olds are taught by professional staff, using a "please touch" approach. Call 370-8276 for a brochure or 322-7009 for space availability.

Related places of interest: *Bald Eagle Days (January); Boulder Creek Festival (May); Channel 4 Education EXPO (March); Colorado Indian Market and Wester Art Roundup (January and July); Conservation Day at the Zoo (June); Dakota Hogback Geological Cross-section Site; Denver Black Arts Festival (July); Dinosaur Ridge Tours; Earth Day Celebrations at the Denver Museum of Natural History (April), at the Collage Children's Museum (April), and at Earthfest (April); Free Day at the Denver Museum of Natural History (September and October); Geology Museum; Henderson Museum of Natural History; March Pow Wow (March); Morrison Museum of Natural History; National Trail Days (June); Rocky Mountain Arsenal National Wildlife Refuge*

FISKE PLANETARIUM

Have you ever wondered what it's like to stand on Mars or ride a comet or whether the moon was made of green cheese? These are just a few of the awesome facts you'll discover when you come to Fiske Planetarium, the largest Planetarium between Chicago and Los Angeles! Come early to the Saturday afternoon show or stay a little later, after the show is over, and see the scale model of the solar system...the part of the universe where Earth is located, along with some other planets, and the sun, of course. The model starts at the entrance to the Planetarium, and continues across Regent Drive. It's planet-tasmik!

Where is it? On the campus of the University of Colorado in Boulder, near Broadway and Regent Drive.

Phone numbers? Information, 492-5001; reservations, 492-5002.

Parking? Drive north on Broadway to Regent Drive. Turn right into the University of Colorado campus, right again at Kittredge Loop and right again at Parking Lot No. 308. The parking is <u>free</u> for those attending Fiske public programs. Metered parking is also available along Regent Drive, next to the Planetarium. Bring change.

Other transportation? RTD buses stop nearby.

Open what days and hours? Fridays, 7:30 p.m.; Saturdays, 2:00 p.m., year-round.

Entrance fees? Fridays: children and senior adults, $1.75; other adults, $3.00; Saturdays: children and senior adults, $1.50; other adults, $2.25.

Star shows? Saturday matinee performances are specifically prepared for children, 4 to 12 years old. The Friday night shows are more adult oriented; and, weather permitting, they are followed by a look through a telescope at the Somers-Bausch Observatory. Don't miss the interactive science displays in the lobby.

Tours? Self-guided tour of the Colorado Scale Model Solar System, which begins outdoors at the Planetarium entrance and continues across Regent Drive.

Related places of interest: Chamberlin Observatory; Charles C. Gates Planetarium; Christmas at Fiske (December)

GEOLOGY MUSEUM

Did you ever wonder what an "old fossil" was? Are you likely to pick up rocks and wonder if there is gold or silver in them? Do gems spark your interest? The Geology Museum abounds with all of the above. You'll even see a recreation of the famous Clear Creek Cave where precious rocks and minerals were discovered! This is a great museum to explore. And before you leave, don't forget to borrow the Fossil Kit and the Mineral Kit. You can spend the next two-weeks learning more in the comfort of your own home. Awesome!

Where is it? At 16th and Maple Streets in Golden, on the Colorado School of Mines campus. Drive west on Sixth Avenue into Golden. Turn right at 19th Street (a traffic light), and then take the first left. Continue to the end to 16th Street and turn right. Drive one more block to Maple Street. The Museum is on the north corner, facing west.
Phone number? 273-3815.
Parking? It's free but you may have trouble finding something. Try the visitor's parking area at the Guggenheim Building, north of the Museum, on Maple Street.
Other transportation? RTD stops nearby.
Open what days and hours? Open Mondays through Saturdays, 9:00 a.m. to 4:00 p.m.; Sundays, 1:00 to 4:00 p.m.
Entrance fees? None. It's free.
Exhibits? There are indoor and outdoor exhibits, all self-guided. The inside exhibits include: minerals from around the world, fossils, earth history, and the geology of the Golden area. Special exhibits: Colorado mining history and equipment, basic geologic concepts, gemstones and

precious metals, the Clear Creek Cave, and the Guild Gold Mine (not yet open). You can reserve and check out for two-weeks, a Fossil Kit and a Mineral Kit, each containing a booklet that guides you through the kit.
Wheelchair accessible? Yes.
Food? Yes.
Restrooms? Yes.

Related places of interest: *Henderson Museum of Natural History; Colorado History Museum; Dakota Hogback Geological Cross-Section Site; Denver Museum of Natural History; Free Day at the Denver Museum of Natural History (September and October); Gold Panning in Clear Creek; Morrison Museum of Natural History rock and gem collection; Dinosaur Ridge Tours; Hiwan Homestead House gem collection*

HENDERSON MUSEUM OF NATURAL HISTORY

Did you ever wonder if you had interesting things to explore outside your own house...like bugs and rocks and bones and foot prints? Well, you might get some really neat ideas when you go to the Henderson Museum of Natural History. They have a place where you can learn what to look for. And, besides, they have lots of interesting things to see in other parts of the Museum, including dinosaurs!

Where is it? On the campus of the University of Colorado, in the Henderson Building, off Broadway and Euclid Street.
Phone number? 492-6892.
Parking? Weekdays: Free on-street parking, or in the Euclid Parking Structure off Broadway on Euclid Street for a fee.

Weekends: <u>Free</u> parking in the Museum parking lot or on the street.

Other transportation? RTD buses and the HOP shuttles stop nearby.

Open what days and hours? Mondays through Fridays, 9:00 a.m. to 5:00 p.m.; Saturdays, 9:00 a.m. to 4:00 p.m.; Sundays, 10 a.m. to 4:00 p.m.

Entrance fees? None. It's <u>free</u>.

Exhibits? On two floors there are several permanent exhibits and one gallery for changing exhibits. The permanent exhibits include a Dinosaur Hall, a Hall of Life, and an Anthropology Hall, with items from the Rocky Mountain and Southwest regions, and a Discovery Corner for children. This Discovery Corner is designed to look like a back yard with many hands-on materials, such as stuffed birds, fossils, rocks, bones, and a microscope. The children are encouraged to examine all that is there. A recent special exhibit dealt with dinosaur tracking.

Wheelchair accessible? Yes.

Food? No.

Restrooms? Yes.

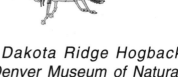

Related places of interest: Dakota Ridge Hogback Geological Cross-section Site; Denver Museum of Natural History; Dinosaur Ridge Tours; Free Day at the Denver Museum of Natural History (September and October); Geology Museum; Morrison Museum of Natural History

MIZEL MUSEUM OF JUDAICA

Did you know that most everybody in Denver has a party when a baby is born or when a child becomes an adult, and when someone gets married? And when someone dies, they grieve with family and friends? Depending on your cultural heritage, the way you recognize these events may be a little different if you are Native American, Hispanic, African American, Asian American, or Jewish. You can find out about these special moments in all of our lives at the Mizel Museum and compare them to the way your family observes them.

Where is it? At 560 South Monaco Street Parkway, in East Denver. Drive east on Sixth Avenue to Monaco Street Parkway and turn right. Continue to Center Avenue and turn left and left again into the east entrance parking lot.
Phone number? 333-4156; ask for Gail Bell.
Parking? Yes, and it's <u>free</u>.
Other transportation? RTD buses stop nearby.
Open what days and hours? Mondays through Thursdays, 10:00 a.m. to 4:00 p.m.; Sundays, 10:00 a.m. to noon.
Entrance fee? None. It's <u>free</u>.
Exhibits? *Bridges of Understanding* is a permanent exhibit which compares four stages involving the rights of passage (birth/naming, childhood to adulthood, marriage, and death), for five Denver cultural groups: Afro-American, Asian-Pacific, Hispanic, Jewish, and Native American Indians. Changing exhibits have included *Immigration to Colorado, 1850 to the Present.*
Tours? They are self-guiding.
Wheelchair accessible? Yes.
Food? Yes.
Restrooms? Yes.

Related places of interest: African Arts Family Day (October); Black American West Museum and Heritage

Center; Cherry Blossom Festival (June); Chile Harvest Festival (August); Cinco de Mayo Celebration (May); Colorado History Museum; Colorado Indian Market and Western Art Roundup (January and July); Denver Black Arts Festival (July); Eulipions Cultural Center; Fiesta! Fiesta! (September); Holiday Open House at Four-Mile Historic Park (December); Japanese Festival (May); Juneteenth Celebration (June); Kwansaa Celebration (December); Lights of December Celebration (December); March Pow-Wow (March); Martin Luther King, Jr., Birthday March (January); Mayor's Tree Lighting (December); Parade of Lights (December); Passport to Asia Festival (August); St. Patrick's Day Parade (March)

MOLLY BROWN HOUSE

Who in the world was Molly Brown? And why would anyone name a house after her? When you visit the Molly Brown house to get the answers to these two questions, you'll learn something about Colorado's early history at the same time. And you'll learn why a musical play was written about this interesting woman.

Where is it? 1340 Pennsylvania Avenue in Denver.
Phone number? 832-4092.
Parking? Yes, and it's <u>free</u> and is on the street; handicapped parking is on the side of the House.
Other transportation? RTD buses and the Cultural Connection Trolley stop nearby.
Open what days and hours? Tuesdays through Saturdays, 10:00 a.m. to 4:00 p.m.; Sundays, 12:00 to 4:00 p.m.; closed Mondays and all major holidays.

Entrance fees? Children under 6 years old, <u>free</u>; 6 to 12 year-olds, $1.50; senior adults over 65, $2.50; other adults, $3.00.

Exhibits? There are two: the furnishings of this 1920s middle-class, Victorian House, and the sinking of the ocean liner, The Titanic.

Tours? Of the Main House and Carriage House, approximately every 20 minutes, with stories about Molly Brown interspersed with commentary on the furnishings.

Wheelchair accessible? Partially.

Food? No.

Restrooms? Yes.

Related places of interest: Belmar Museum and Historic Village; Black American West Museum and Cultural Center; Boulder History Museum; Colorado History Museum; Denver History Museum and the Byers-Evans House; Denver Museum of Miniatures, Dolls, and Toys; Four-Mile Historic Park; Hiwan Homestead House; Littleton Historical Museum

MORRISON MUSEUM OF NATURAL HISTORY

Just think...stegasauruses roamed around Morrison many, many, many years ago. Isn't that cool? At the Morrison Museum of Natural History, you can see the first stegosaurus that was found in Morrison, and you can even help to dig out some bones if you get there at the right time. This is where it's at!

Where is it? One half mile south of Morrison on Highway 8.

Phone number? 697-1873.

Parking? Yes, and it's <u>free</u>.
Other transportation? No.
Open what days and hours? Wednesdays through Sundays, 1:00 to 4:00 p.m.
Exhibits? There is a real work station in progress on the first level, where bones of a stegosaurus are being removed from rocks that were found in this area. At times, children can take part in this work. There are also exhibits and a videotape which describes Dinosaur Ridge, located just three miles from the Museum. Another exhibit shows baby dinosaurs and the eggs from which they hatched. One part of the Museum is an old cabin that was found on a nearby ranch and renovated. It houses an exhibit of fossils from around the world.
Tours? Guided tours are possible when it's not too busy.
Entrance fees? None. It's <u>free</u>.
Wheelchair accessible? Yes.
Food? No.
Restrooms? Yes.

Related places of interest: *Dakota Hogback Geological Cross-Section; Denver Museum of Natural History; Dinosaur Ridge Tours; Free Day at the Denver Museum of Natural History (September and October); Geology Museum; Henderson Museum of Natural History*

NATIONAL CENTER FOR ATMOSPHERIC RESEARCH (NCAR)

Are you wondering what an Atmospheric Research Center does? Its a place where people study all about the air around the earth, here in Boulder and everywhere else in the world. These scientists try to discover how and why there is rain, sleet, snow, tornados, hurricanes, tidal waves, thunder, and lightening. They have many different kinds of tools to get information from the air, the sun, the oceans, and the clouds...and even from termites! Some of these tools are shown in the lobby of NCAR'S Mesa Laboratory and you can make some of the weather happen right there. Wouldn't it be cool to learn more about the weather?

The National Center for Atmospheric Research and the Flatirons.
Photo: NCAR/UCAR/NSF

129

Where is it? At West Table Mesa Drive in south-western Boulder. Drive south on Broadway to South Boulder Road, turn right and continue out to where it becomes Table Mesa Drive. Stay on Table Mesa Drive to the NCAR parking lot.

Phone numbers? 497-1174 or 497-1173.

Parking? Yes, and it's <u>free</u>.

Other transportation? RTD buses stop nearby but run infrequently. Call 443-0100 for times.

Open what days and hours? Mondays through Fridays, 8:00 a.m. to 5:00 p.m.; Saturdays, Sundays, and holidays, 9:00 a.m. to 3:00 p.m.

Entrance fees? No. It's <u>free</u>.

Exhibits? NCAR is famous for its studies of weather, climate, the chemistry of the atmosphere, and the sun. There are seven hands-on exhibits, exact replicas of the Exploritorium Exhibit at the San Francisco Museum. For example, if you follow the directions, you'll be able to make a tornado, cause fog, create lightening, generate air turbulence, and show chaotic weather patterns. Besides being a lot of fun, it may help you to understand how and why weather happens. Don't miss seeing the giant 18 foot super computer in the basement. It helps the researchers to look at all the information they gather from around the world. It can solve two million problems a second. Pretty smart!

Tours? <u>Free</u> guided and self-guided tours. In the summer (end of June to beginning of September), guided tours are offered Mondays through Fridays at noon. In the winter, they are on Saturdays at noon. Self-guided tours are available year-round. Information on self-guided tours is at the kiosk in NCAR's lobby.

Wheelchair accessible? Yes.

Food? In NCAR's cafeteria.

Restrooms? Yes.

130

Related places of interest: *Boulder Airport; Centennial Airport; Channel 4 Education EXPO (March); Children's Museum; Denver International Airport; Forest Fire-Fighter Center; National Earthquake Center; Rocky Mountain Air Fair (September); Wings Over the Rockies Aviation and Space Museum*

NATIONAL EARTHQUAKE CENTER

Did you think that the word "crust," had to do with a piece of bread...and that "trembling" or "shaking" is what you do when you're scared...and that "fault" means you did something wrong? If so, then these four words will take on a new meaning for you when you visit the National Earthquake Center. That's where they study earthquakes around the world, not just in the United States. In fact, the Center records earthquakes as far away as the South China Sea! When you take their tour, you'll find out how they record the "trembling" and "shaking" under the earth's "crust" when underground volcanoes erupt and underground rocks break and shift and cause "faults". It's awesome!

Where is it? At 1711 Illinois Street, on the Colorado School of Mines campus in Golden.
Phone number? 238-1500.
Parking? Yes, and it's <u>free</u>.
Other transportation? RTD buses stop nearby.
Open when? Call for an appointment to take the tour at least six weeks in advance.
Entrance fees? None. It's <u>free</u>.
Tours? Yes, for those 11 years old and older. They last for about one hour.

Wheelchair accessible? Yes.
Food? No.
Restrooms? Yes.

Related places of interest: National Center for Atmospheric Research

UNITED STATES MINT

Did you ever think money grew on trees? Well, you'll change your mind when you hear the thumping of presses and the jingle of coins as they roll out of the machines at the United States Mint in downtown Denver. I'm not talking about some kind of candy money, either; this is the real thing, and Denver and Philadelphia are the only two cities in all of the United States where coins are made. After you finish the tour, answer this question: Which of the following words best describes a person who collects coins?

Banker, Miser, Numismatist, Skinflint, Economist, Tightwad, Saver, or Cheapskate

Where is it? At 320 West Colfax Avenue at Cherokee Street in downtown Denver.
Phone number? 844-3582.
Parking? Metered parking is where you find it so bring along plenty of change.
Other transportation? RTD buses and the Cultural Connection Trolley stop nearby.
Open what days and hours? Weekdays only, 8:00 a.m. to 3:00 p.m., except Wednesdays when it opens at 9:00 a.m.; closed, weekends and holidays.

Entrance fees? None. Tours are <u>free</u>.
Tour? The 15 minute tour covers the entire production of coins, from stamping to counting and bagging.
Exhibits? "Money, Trade, and Treasures," a look at historic coins, money, and trade.
Wheelchair accessible? Yes.
Food? No.
Restrooms? Yes.

Related places of interest: Boulder Daily Camera; Celestial Seasoning Tea Company;

UNIVERSITY OF COLORADO HERITAGE CENTER

Did you know that there were 12 astronauts who graduated from the University of Colorado? They gave some of the stuff they used on their space missions to this museum for you to see. You also can see the first model for the University of Colorado in Boulder. Some of the buildings in the model were never built. Can you locate Old Main, were the Heritage Center is located? This is a small museum with big things to see.

Where is it? On the campus of the University of Colorado in Boulder; the third floor of Old Main. The closest intersection is Broadway and University Avenue. Walk on campus from University Avenue. Old Main is across from Varsity Pond.
Phone number? 492-6329.
Parking? Metered, on-street parking on University Avenue or the side streets. Bring change.
Other transportation? RTD buses and the HOP shuttle stop nearby.

Open what days and hours? Tuesdays through Fridays, 10:00 a.m. to 4:00 p.m.

Entrance fees? None. It's <u>free</u>.

Exhibits? You'll see space suits and other artifacts of space travel that were used by the astronauts who graduated from the University of Colorado. There is also an athletic room with photographs of the old Colorado University teams and some trophies they won. The Architectural Gallery shows the original model of the University campus.

Tours? These can be arranged in advance or you can guide yourself through the exhibits.

Wheelchair accessible? Yes.

Food? No.

Restrooms? Yes.

Related places of interest: Wings Over the Rockies Aviation and Space Museum; games played by the Colorado University Buffalos Football Team and Basketball Teams

WINGS OVER THE ROCKIES AVIATION AND SPACE MUSEUM

Would you like to walk through a space station? You can, by going to Wings Over the Rockies Aviation and Space Museum. The space station was built to be sent into outer-space but came to the Museum instead. Doesn't it make you wonder what it would be like working and living inside this station so far away from earth?

Where is it? In Building 401 (Hangar No. 1), at 7985 East Irvington Place in Denver. Drive east on 14th Avenue to Quebec Street and turn right. Continue on Quebec Street to

1st Avenue and the entry gate. Tell the guards you are going to the Museum and they'll provide you with a pass and directions.

Phone number? 360-5360.

Parking? Yes, and it's <u>free</u>.

Other transportation? RTD buses stop nearby.

Open what days and hours? Daily, 10:00 a.m. to 5:00 p.m.; closed Thanksgiving, Christmas, and New Year's Days.

Entrance fees? Children under 5 years old and members, <u>free</u>; children over 5, students with ID, senior adults 65 and over, $2.00.

Exhibits? This new Museum opened December 1st, 1994, with just the bare beginnings of what it hopes to be in 1995 and beyond. They have in place the Lowry Heritage Museum collection of 20 military aircraft, including a B1 bomber and a B2 fuselage cutaway. They are installing a walk-through cylindrical space station which is 16 feet by 45 feet and built for a space launch by Martin-Marietta Company. And they are expecting exhibit donations from Bradley Air Force Base and the United States Airforce Academy in Colorado Springs.

Tours? Self-guiding, only.

Wheelchair accessible? Yes.

Food? Yes.

Restrooms? Yes.

Related places of interest: Boulder Airport; Centennial Airport; Denver International Airport; University of Colorado Heritage Museum; Forest Fire-Fighter Center; One Sky, One World International Kite Fly (October); Rocky Mountain Air Fair (September); University of Colorado Heritage Center

INDOOR-OUTDOOR MUSEUMS

BARR LAKE STATE PARK NATURE CENTER

Don't you just love being outdoors where the creepy-crawly critters and slimy slugs make their homes along with the birds, the bees, and the bunnies? The Barr Lake Nature Center is just the place to be, summer or winter, because there's always something going on, indoors and outdoors...like hunting for four-legged footprints and looking for your many-feathered friends...like calling wild flowers by name and learning about why the leaves change color in the fall. Find out about all the fun things you can do there and do them!

Where is it? At 13401 Picadilly Road in Brighton. Drive north in Route I-25 and exit to Route I-76 going east. Continue to Bromley Lane, Exit 22, and take a right turn on Bromley. When you get to Picadilly Road, turn right and drive about 2 miles to the Park entrance.
Phone number? 659-6005.
Parking? Yes, and it's free.
Other transportation? No.
Open what days and hours? Park: Year-round, 5:00 a.m. to 10:00 p.m. Nature Center: Year-round, Wednesdays to Sundays; winters, 9:00 a.m. to 4:00 p.m.; summers, 8:00 a.m. to 5:00 p.m.
Entrance fees? $3.00 to enter the Park; the activities are free.
Programs? Nature programs for children include slide shows, hikes, arts and crafts activities, with more frequent programs during the summer than winter months. Some past programs included: *Beautiful Bunnies, Marvelous Muskrats, Colors in Leaves,* and *Giving Thanks to Wildlife.*

Wheelchair accessible? Yes.
Food? No.
Restrooms? Yes.

Related places of interest: Bald Eagle Days (January);
Denver Museum of Natural History; Lookout Mountain
Nature Center; National Center for Atmospheric Research;
National Trail Days (June); Rocky Mountain Arsenal National
Wildlife Refuge

BELMAR MUSEUM AND HISTORIC VILLAGE

Did you know that many, many years ago, there were
farms here and farms there, that farms were simply everywhere in Lakewood? If you're curious, you'll want to see
what one of these farms looked like and the kind of schools
kids used to go to in those "good old days." Just head for
Belmar Museum and Historic Village. You can walk through
an old farm house, barn, and school house and see old trac-
tors and farm tools on display. And, after a lot of looking
around, you can take a stroll to the lakes and see the ducks
and geese...and maybe even a blue heron. Then, take a
guided or self-guided walk on the nature trails. It's a great
place to go for the day!

Where is it? At 797 South Wadsworth Boulevard, near the
Villa Italia Shopping Center, in Belmar Park, Lakewood.
Phone numbers? Information, 987-7031; reservations,
987-7850.
Parking? Yes, and it's <u>free</u>.
Other transportation? RTD buses stop nearby.
Open what days and hours? Mondays through Fridays,

10:00 a.m. to 4:00 p.m.; Saturdays, 1:00 to 5:00 p.m.; closed, Sundays.

Entrance fees? None. It's <u>free</u>.

Exhibits? Lakewood's past and present are exhibited in this Museum. You can uncover them by exploring a "Discovery Trunk" and a pre-electric era farmhouse, barn, and country schoolhouse, all furnished as they were in the old days. The Park includes 127 acres of gardens, two lakes, and several nature trails. One such trail is wheelchair accessible, covers 1½ miles, and is self-guiding.

Tours? "Trunk" programs must be arranged in advance by making reservations. There are guided tours of the old buildings.

Wheelchair accessible? Partially.

Food? Only with special annual events; see Chapter 6.

Horse and Wagon Ride.
Photo: Lakewood's Historical Belmar Village

However, there is a snack bar next door in the Municipal Building.
Restrooms? Yes.

Related places of interest: Aurora History Museum; Arvada History Museum and Art Gallery; Cider Days (October); Denver History Museum and the Byers-Evans House; Denver Museum of Miniatures, Dolls, and Toys; Four Mile Historical Park; Littleton Historical Museum

BOULDER AIRPORT

Coming here is the next best thing to flying your own plane! Starting with a visit to the Control Tower, you can learn how to plan your flight, using all the information from the map and computer. Then, hop in your plane, establish radio communication, and take off into the clear, blue Colorado skies. This is where it's at!

Where is it? 3300 Airport Road, Building J, in Boulder. Drive on Colorado Route 157 (Foothills Highway) to Velmont Road and turn right. Continue about half-a-mile to Airport Road. At the top of the curve, make a left turn into the Airport to Building J.
Phone number? 440-7065
Parking? Yes.
Other transportation? No.
Open what days and hours? By appointment; call Ray Grundy, the Airport Manager.
Tour? Mr. Grundy makes this experience as "hands-on" as possible. The tour includes the flight planning area which has a large map with distances marked in nautical miles, the

computer that provides the pilots with weather information, and the radio used to communicate with the pilots. You'll also see some of the small planes, sit in one, and handle the controls, with Mr. Grundy explaining about how things work.
Entrance fees? None. It's <u>free</u>.
Wheelchair accessible? Yes.
Food? No.
Restrooms? Yes.

Related places of interest: Centennial Airport; Children's Museum; Denver International Airport; Forest Fire-Fighter Center; One Sky, One World International Kite Fly (October); Rocky Mountain Air Fair (September); Wings Over the Rockies Aviation and Space Museum

Buffalo Bill.
Photo: *Buffalo Bill Memorial Museum*

BUFFALO BILL'S MEMORIAL MUSEUM AND GRAVE

Did you know that Buffalo Bill Cody was a Pony Express rider, an Army scout, a buffalo hunter, and a great show man? Did you know that his show became so famous around the world that he was invited to perform before queens and kings? This Museum exhibit tells you all about Buffalo Bill's life and all about his Wild West Shows and the "cowgirls" who helped to make his show famous, like Annie Oakley and Goldie Griffith. Just outside the Museum, at a point overlooking Denver and the plains beyond, is the place where Buffalo Bill was buried.

This is a great place to find out the facts about one of the most famous cowboys of them all. And, you can celebrate Buffalo Bill's birthday every year at the Museum on February 26th.

Where is it? On top of Lookout Mountain on Route 5 in Golden. Take Route I-70 to Exit 256.
Phone number? 526-0747.
Parking? Yes, and it's <u>free</u>.
Other transportation? No.
Open what days and hours? Daily, 9:00 a.m. to 5:00 p.m.
Entrance fees? Children under 6 years old, <u>free</u>; youth 6 to 12, $1.00; senior adults, $1.50; other adults $2.00.
Wheelchair accessible? Yes.
Food? Yes,
Restrooms? Yes.

Related places of interest: *Adams County Fair and Rodeo (August); Black American West Museum and Heritage Center; Buffalo Bill's Birthday Celebration (February);*

*Buffalo Bill Days (July); Colorado History Museum; Denver
Art Museum Western Art Exhibit; Denver Museum of Natural
History Native American Indian Exhibit; National Western
Stock Show and Rodeo (January)*

CENTENNIAL AIRPORT

Did you know that there are big, medium-sized, and
small airports around Denver? The only ones that let you
find out about the inside workings are the small ones...for
safety reasons. At Centennial Airport, you can learn about
different kinds of airports, visit the control tower, and climb
into a small plane, if you're lucky. If you use your imagina-
tion, you'll even be able to fly.

Where is it? 7800 South Peoria Street in Englewood. Drive
south on Route I-25 and exit at Arapahoe Road. Continue
east on Arapahoe Road to Peoria Street; then go south to
the end of the road.
Phone number? 790-0598.
Parking? Yes, and it's <u>free</u>.
Other transportation? No.
Open what days and hours? Everyday, by appointment. In
case of an emergency or bad weather conditions, the tour
may be canceled. Call Don Ulane to schedule a time, one to
two weeks in advance and check back on the day of your
tour.
Tour? This tour is limited to children over eight years old.
You are shown a slide show about the work of this airport as
compared to others. You visit the control tower, and you may
look at and climb inside a plane, if one is available.
Entrance fees? None. It's <u>free</u>.

Wheelchair accessible? Partially.
Food? Yes, and there's a place to picnic and watch the planes.
Restrooms? Yes.

Related places of interest: Boulder Airport; Denver International Airport; Forest Fire-Fighter Center; One Sky, One World International Kite Fly (October); Rocky Mountain Air Fair (September)

DENVER BOTANIC GARDENS

When there are no flowers blooming and the grass looks more brown than green and the trees have no leaves...do you ever wish it was spring or summer? If so, go for a slow walk through the green house at the Denver Botanic Gardens. You'll be surrounded by trees of all sizes, with green leaves of many shapes, and you'll even see flowers of different colors. Sniff the air. It smells like summer after a rain storm. And when spring and summer do arrive, enjoy meandering around the outdoor gardens. You'll be delighted by all the colors, shapes, and sizes the flowers come in. Remember, sniff the air. It's could smell like dozens of perfume bottles being opened at the same time. Wow!

Where is it? At 1005 York Street in Denver.
Phone number? 331-4000.
Parking? Yes, and it's <u>free</u>.
Other transportation? RTD buses and the Cultural Connection Trolley stop nearby.
Open what days and hours? Everyday, 9:00 a.m. to 5:00 p.m. and until 8:00 p.m. in December.

Entrance fees? Children 15 and under, $1.00; students with I.D. and senior adults, $1.50; other adults $3.00.

Exhibits? There are outdoor gardens of native and exotic plants; Japanese, rose, herb, and rock gardens; and a tropical conservatory (green house) that you can walk through. There are also special exhibits scheduled throughout the year.

Wheelchair accessible? Yes.

Food? No.

Restrooms? Yes.

Related places of interest: Belmar Park; Chatfield Arboretum; Chile Harvest Festival (August); Denver Black Arts Festival (July); Herald the Season (December); Japanese Festival (June)

DENVER INTERNATIONAL AIRPORT (D.I.A.)

This is a very big airport...the newest one in the world, and it's truly awesome! The roof is supposed to remind you of Colorado's snow-capped mountains. I think they look like tents or the tops of ice-cream cones. What do you think? You can get a great view of these mountains and of planes taking off and landing, any time of the year, from inside the airport by looking through a huge wall of glass. And there are several ways to get around this very big Airport. You can take short train rides from one concourse to another; you can be carried on a moving walkway within a concourse; and you can take elevators or escalators, up or down, from one level to another. You can even climb up and down stairs. And if you want to discover what an "atrium" is, you can go to the top of one and look down into it. Don't miss a visit to D.I.A.

Where is it? At the east end of Peña Boulevard, Denver. It is accessed from Route I-70 and Tower Road.

Phone number? 342-2200.

Parking? In garages for a fee paid at a toll booth when you leave.

Other transportation? RTD "Sky Ride," which consists of six lines originating from Boulder Transit Center, Denver Federal Center, Civic Center Station, Stapleton Transit Center, Northglenn Transit Center, and Arapahoe Road Park-n-Ride.

Open what days and hours? Daily.

What can be seen? Jeppesen Terminal (named after an aviation pioneer) has a translucent, Teflon-coated, fiberglass roof designed to evoke the snow-capped mountains. An elevated walkway encircles and overlooks an atrium. A massive

Denver International Airport - Jeppeson Terminal.

Photo: D.I.A.

glass wall provides a breathtaking view of the Rocky Mountains and airport flight activity. There are automated trains that link the terminal with the three concourses. Each of the concourses have moving walkways.

Tours? It is due to open in February of 1995, after several delays. Tours are self-guided in public areas only.

Wheelchair accessible? Yes.

Food? Yes.

Restrooms? Yes.

Related places of interest: Boulder Airport; Centennial Airport; Forest Fire-Fighter Center; Open Sky, One World International Kite Fly (October); Rocky Mountain Air Fair (September); Wings Over the Rockies Aviation and Space Museum

FOREST FIRE-FIGHTER CENTER

Smokey the Bear is alive and well at the Forest Fire-Fighter Center. I bet you'd love to see the airport where the women and men take off to fight forest fires in Colorado. Did you ever wonder how they did it? What their equipment looked like? What the inside of the plane looked like? You can take a tour of this amazing place just by calling ahead of time. Don't miss it!

Where is it? At the Jefferson County Airport in Broomfield. Take Route I-25 north to the Boulder Turnpike Exit (Route 36). Drive on the Turnpike and take the Lafayette-Broomfield Exit (Route 287) and turn left at the top of the ramp. Drive to the second traffic light and turn right on to Route 128 for about 200 yards and turn left and then right on to Frontage

Road (120th Avenue). Continue on this road to the Rocky Mountain Coordination Center, U.S. Forest Service, a large green building on the left.

Phone number? 275-5710.

Parking? Yes, and it's <u>free</u>.

Open what days and hours? Winter: Mondays through Fridays, 8:00 a.m. to 4:30 p.m.; late April to late September, everyday, 8:00 a.m. to 4:30 p.m.

Entrance fees? None. It's <u>free</u>.

Tours? All tours are <u>free</u> and take about an hour. Call to arrange a day and time.

Exhibits? The clothing and equipment worn by fire fighters; the Dispatch Center where fire-fighters and supervisors are assembled; storage tanks with fire retardants used by the planes; aircraft to fight fires. Children may be allowed to get in a plane if it's not too busy.

Wheelchair accessible? Yes.

Food? No.

Restrooms? Yes.

Wheelchair accessible? Yes.

Food? No.

Restrooms? Yes.

Related places of interest: *Boulder Airport; Centennial Airport, Denver Fire-Fighters Museum; Denver International Airport; Rocky Mountain Air Fair (September); Wings Over the Rockies Aviation and Space Museum*

FORNEY TRANSPORTATION MUSEUM

If the first word you spoke was "car," instead of "daddy" or "mommy," this is the museum for you. Or if you love seeing cars on the road or trains on the track, this is the museum for you. Or if you think anything with wheels on it is great stuff, this is the museum for you. There are over 300 cars, carriages, bicycles, steam engines, railroad cars and other kinds of transportation for you to see, both inside and outside the museum. You can climb in the cab of the 1906 Steam Locomotive, but everything else is to be looked at and not touched. "Big Boy" is the name of the world's largest steam locomotive and the Museum is very proud to have one of the 25 that was built back in 1941. Going to this Museum is a truly moving experience.

Where is it? At 1416 Platte Street in Denver. Take Exit 211 off Route I-25, and drive five blocks east.
Phone number? 433-3643.
Parking? Yes, and it's free.
Other transportation? RTD buses, the Cultural Connection Trolley, and the Platte Valley Trolley stop nearby.
Open what days and hours? Mondays through Saturdays, 10:00 a.m. to 5:00 p.m.; Sundays, 11:00 a.m. to 5:00 p.m.; closed on Thanksgiving, Christmas, and New Year's Day.
Entrance fees? Children 5 years old and under, free; those between 6 and 12 years old, $2.00; between 12 and 18 years old, $3.00; adults, $4.00.
Wheelchair accessible? No.
Food? No.
Restrooms? No.

Related places of interest: Celebration of 1860s Work and Play (April); Colorado Railroad Museum; Denver Auto Show (February); Denver International Airport; Denver Zoo's Miniature Train Ride; Holiday Open House at Four-Mile Historic Park (December); Kinetic Conveyance Parade (April); Kinetic Conveyance Race (May); Lakeside Amusement Park's Miniature Train Ride; Lion's Club Miniature Train Ride; Model Railroad at the Union Pacific Railroad Station; Organic Fair (September); Tiny Town Miniature Train Ride; Tri-State Auto Show (March)

FOUR-MILE HISTORIC PARK

Did you ever read about the old days, when the pioneers first came to Denver and built themselves houses from whole tree trunks? And did you read about how people worked on their farms and traveled in stage coaches and stayed at inns? Well, those old days are there for you to see with your own eyes at the Four-Mile Historic Park. It used to be a stage coach stop. And the log house is the oldest house in Denver. There's so much for you to see and learn here just by walking around and asking questions. And, if you're not careful, you'll probably have a lot of fun doing it.

Where is it? At 715 South Forest Street in Denver.
Phone number? 399-1859.
Parking? Yes, and it's <u>free</u>.
Other transportation? RTD buses stop nearby.
Open what days and hours? Open April through September, Wednesdays through Sundays, 10:00 a.m. to 4:00 p.m., except for Special Events. (See Chapter 6, *Looking Ahead*). Closed Mondays and Tuesdays.

Entrance fees? Children under 6 years old, <u>free</u>; 6 to 15 year-olds and senior adults over 65, $2.00; other adults, $3.50.

Exhibits? The oldest house in Denver, made with the original hand-hewn logs back in 1859. It is on a 12-acre farm with a stage coach stop, tavern, and inn. During their Special Events Days in April, July, September, October, and December (see Chapter 6, *Looking Ahead*), this is a living history museum, featuring old fashioned foods and costumed farm folk working at farming, blacksmithing, quilting, spinning, lace making, gold panning, and butter churning. All visitors have a chance to ride the stagecoach, hay wagon, or sleigh.

Tours? A tour of the historic house with a costumed guide. Self-guided tours of the farmstead where you will see the

Stage Coach Ride.

Photo: Four-Mile Historic Park

draft horses, chickens, and crops.
Wheelchair accessible? Limited.
Food? Only at special events. You can picnic here, however.
Restrooms? Yes.
Birthday parties? Yes.

Related places of interest: Aurora History Museum; Arvada History Museum and Art Gallery; Belmar Museum and Historic Village; Black American West Museum and Heritage Center; Boulder History Museum; Colorado History Museum; Celebration of 1860s Work and Play (April); Denver History Museum and the Byers-Evans House; Gold Panning in Clear Creek; Hiwan Homestead Museum; Holiday Open House at Four-Mile Historic Park (December); Old-fashioned Fourth of July Family Picnic (July); Organic Fair (September); Spirits of the Past (October)

HIWAN HOMESTEAD MUSEUM

Coming to this Museum gives you a good idea about the kinds of houses some people lived in a long, long time ago, when the pioneers first began to settle out here. You'll also be surprised to find a big saddle that you can climb on in the old stone house. Its just like the ones cowboys used to put on their horses and sit in when they went out to round up the cattle. You could even pretend that you're a cowgirl or cowboy and maybe even sing the famous Gene Autry song, "I'm back in the saddle again."

Where is it? Travel west from Denver on Route I-70 and take the Evergreen Exit #252. Continue for 6½ miles towards Evergreen, until you see the sign for the Hiwan Homestead

Museum. Turn left on Douglas Park Road and drive another ½ mile to the Museum, where the road name has changed to Meadow Drive.

Phone number? 674-6262.

Parking? Yes, and it's <u>free</u>.

Other transportation? RTD buses stop nearby but not frequently.

Open what days and hours? Tuesdays through Sundays, 11:00 a.m. to 5:00 p.m.; closed Mondays.

Entrance fees? None. It's <u>free</u>.

Exhibits? Consists of several restored 19th century buildings, including a seventeen-room log home. The stone house has a rock and gem collection and a cowboy exhibit where children can sit on a horse saddle.

Wheelchair accessible? Yes.

Food? No.

Restrooms? Yes.

Related places of interest: Aurora History Museum; Arvada History Museum and Art Gallery; Belmar Museum and Historic Village; Black American West Museum and Heritage Center; Boulder History Museum; D.A.R. Pioneer Museum; Denver History Museum and the Byers-Evans House; Four-Mile Historic Park; Hiwan House; Littleton Historical Museum; Molly Brown House; National Western Stock Show and Rodeo (January)

LITTLETON HISTORICAL MUSEUM

You may have to pinch yourself when you come to this Museum. You might think you'd traveled into the past. Everything looks exactly like it did 80 or 100 years ago. Even the people who work on the farms are wearing the same 80 or 100-year-old style clothes and using 80 or 100-year-old type tools, that includes the farmers and the blacksmiths. Did you notice the differences between the two farms? Which one would you like to live on?

Where is it? At 6028 South Gallup Avenue and Littleton Boulevard in Littleton.
Phone number? 795-3950.
Parking? Yes, and it's <u>free</u>.
Other transportation? RTD buses stop nearby.
Open what days and hours? Mondays through Fridays, 8:00 a.m. to 5:00 p.m.; Saturdays, 10:00 a.m. to 5:00 p.m.; Sundays 1:00 to 5:00 p.m., year-round, except on major holidays.
Entrance fees? None. It's <u>free</u>.
Exhibits? This Museum includes two operating farms, one from the 1860s and the other from the 1890s, a working Blacksmith's Shop from 1903, a functioning 1860s one-room, log school house, and a 1910 ice house where ice was harvested from Lake Ketring, cut, and then sold. Everything is historically accurate, from the animals, to the clothes worn by the people and the equipment they use. For example, the 1860s farm has oxen, draft horses, sheep, and various kinds of poultry, while the 1890s farm has Jersey milk cows, carriage horses, pigs, and various breeds of poultry. There is a sharp contrast between the two farms which dramatically demonstrates the impact of the coming of the railroad to Littleton. You may walk around the farms and buildings, look at what is going on, and ask questions of any of the workers.

There are three galleries in the main museum building, which have rotating exhibits.

Wheelchair accessible? Yes.
Food? No.
Restrooms? Yes.

Related places of interest: Aurora History Museum; Arvada History Museum and Art Gallery; Belmar Museum and Historic Village; Belleview Park Children's Farm; Black American West History Museum and Cultural Center; Boulder History Museum; Colorado History Museum; D.A.R. Pioneer Museum; Denver History Museum and the Byers-Evans House; Four-Mile Historic Park; Hiwan House; Molly Brown House; Old-fashioned Fourth of July Family Picnic (July); Rocky Mountain Pet EXPO (November)

LOOKOUT MOUNTAIN NATURE CENTER

This would be a great place to have in your own back yard! If you're between 5 and 10 years old, and you can't think of what to do after school, the Nature Center has an After School Special just for you and your friends. You'll discover which creepy-crawly creatures live under those rocks, why the leaves change color before they fall off trees, how to build a bird feeder, or how to create crystals. You may even learn about things you never ever thought about before.

And if you have a kid sister or brother under 5 years old, there's a program for them, too. They can just toddle over there, keep out of your things, and have fun.

I bet you and your family will think the Adventure Pack Program is neat. You can each borrow a backpack filled with activities and equipment, like a compass, thermometer, magnifying lens, wind gauge, and bug boxes. Put the packs on your back, go out on the trails, and explore on your own.

You might want to bring along some trail food and a bottle of water, too.

Where is it? This Jefferson County Open Space Park and Nature Center, is at 910 Colorow Road in Golden, at the top of Lookout Mountain, a five-minute drive from Exit 256 off Route I-70. Follow the brown and white signs to the Jefferson County Conference and Nature Center.
Phone numbers? 526-0594; hearing impaired, 271-5926.
Parking? Yes, and it's <u>free</u>.
Other transportation? No.
Open what days and hours? Tuesdays through Sundays, 10:00 a.m. to 4:00 p.m.
Programs? Call and ask them to mail you a quarterly news letter containing a description of their programs and a schedule of events.
Fees? None. It's <u>free</u> to families and individuals, but you must register 48 hours in advance.
Wheelchair accessible? Yes.
Food? No.
Restrooms? Yes.

Related places of interest: Bald Eagle Days (January); Barr Lake State Park Nature Center; Celebration of 1860s Work and Play (April); Daniels Park Wildlife Preserve; Denver Museum of Natural History; Genesee Park Buffalo and Elk Ranch; Henderson Museum of Natural History; Morrison Museum of Natural History; National Center for Atmospheric Research: Nature Trails; National Trail Days (June); Organic Fair (September)

UNION PACIFIC RAILROAD STATION

Did I hear you ask, "What can I do at a railroad station?" Well, the answer is: You can see where tickets are sold and where trains come in and go out. You can talk to the ticket agent and the conductor, and maybe even the engineer. You can find the engine, the coaches, the dining car, and the baggage car. You can wave goodbye to the passengers. You can sit on a bench and read a time-table and plan a trip. You can buy a train ticket and take a train ride. And, you can come by on a Tuesday night and watch the model railroad run on the Station's lower level.

Where is it? At 1860 Blake Street in lower downtown Denver.
Phone numbers? Train arrivals, 534-2812; AMTRAK, 1-800-872-7245, destinations, times, and ticket reservations.
Parking? Yes, and it's <u>free</u>.
Other transportation? RTD buses stop nearby.
Open what days and hours? 6:00am to 10:00pm
Exhibits? The Model Railroad is on the lower level of the terminal building and runs the last Friday of every month at 7:00 p.m.
Roundtrip somewhere? To Winter Park everyday, leaving Denver at 9:10 a.m. and arriving in Winter Park at 11:05 a.m. Return train to Denver leaves at 4:56 p.m. and arrives at 7:40 p.m. Roundtrip ticket prices range from $38.00 to $50.00; two children traveling with one paying adult each pay half fare. There's a dining car and rest rooms.
Wheelchair accessible? Yes.
Food? Yes.
Restrooms? Yes.

Related places of interest: Colorado Railroad Museum; Forney Transportation Museum; Lakewood Amusement Park Miniature Train Ride; Lion's Club Train Ride at Belleview Park; Tiny Town Miniature Train Ride; Denver Zoo Miniature Train Ride

OUTDOOR MUSEUMS

DAKOTA HOGBACK GEOLOGICAL CROSS-SECTION SITE

This is an awesome sight! You can see many different layers of colored rock up close, as you start your trip westward out of Denver into the Rocky Mountains. Climb up the Hogback and look at the plains to the east and the mountains to the west. Then walk along the trail that brings those layers of rock close enough to see and touch. This rock face was formed by a great push upwards through the earth's crust at sharp angles.

Where is it? Off Route I-70, near Highway 40 at the Morrison interchange, close to Golden.
Phone number? None
Parking? Yes, and it's free.
Other transportation? No.
Open what days and hours? Dawn to dusk, year-round.
Entrance fees? None. It's free.
Exhibits? A walk along the path next to the rock face to get a close-up view of this geological wonder.
Wheelchair accessible? No.
Food? No.
Restrooms? No.

Related places of interest: *Chautauqua Park Rock Formations; Denver Museum of Natural History Rock and Fossil Exhibit; Dinosaur Ridge; Geology Museum; Morrison Museum of Natural History; National Earthquake Center*

DINOSAUR RIDGE TOURS

Isn't it amazing! Dinosaurs roamed throughout Colorado, including the Denver area, many, many years ago. If you want to place your feet closer to where the dinosaurs did, take a trip to Dinosaur Ridge. You'll see bones from a Stegosaurus, dinosaur footprints, plant fossils, animal fossils, signs of the ocean and a mangrove swamp that were once here, and unusual rock shapes jutting at strange angles to the ground. And, if you haven't been to the Morrison Museum of Natural History first, you'll want to go there next. You can help remove dinosaur bones from rocks and see a video-tape about Dinosaur Ridge Then, how about a trip to the Dinosaur Exhibit at Denver's Natural History Museum and a snack in the T-Rex Cafe? This sounds like "dinosaur-mania"!

Where is it? At 16831 West Alameda Parkway in Morrison. Take Route C-470 west to the Morrison Exit. Drive north on the frontage road (Rooney Road), past Vandemeer Speedway, to Alameda Parkway. Turn west on the Parkway and you will see the Ridge in front of you. The Visitor's Center is in a small stone house and barn on the right.
Phone number? 697-3466.
Parking? Yes, and it's <u>free</u>.
Other transportation? No.
Open what days and hours? From April to October, one

day each month is designated *Open Ridge Day*, and no traffic is allowed. Buses run to the ridge every 15 minutes between 10:00 a.m. and 3:00 p.m., and guides take you to 15 points of interest. Year-round, private tours are given, weather permitting. Call 697-3266 for an appointment and information on the cost.

Entrance fees? On Open Ridge Day, children under 2 years old, <u>free</u>; all others, $2.00.

Wheelchair accessible? Partially.

Food? No.

Restrooms? The porta-potty variety.

Related places of interest: Henderson Museum of Natural History; Morrison Museum of Natural History; Denver Museum of Natural History Prehistoric Journey Exhibit; Geology Museum

GOLD PANNING IN CLEAR CREEK

Have you ever had "gold fever"? The people who came out west long ago to find gold had it. They kept hoping they'd strike gold no matter how many times they failed to discover any. One of the places they looked for gold was in stream beds, where the gold was washed down from the mountains into the creeks by the melting snow. You can still search for gold in Clear Creek and maybe even find some. Be careful, though. You might catch "gold fever".

Where is it? Along Route 6 in Clear Creek Canyon, between Golden and Idaho Springs, and along the north fork of Clear Creek.

Phone number? None; drive out and stop at various roadside stands to rent equipment and get lessons.

Parking? Yes, and it's <u>free</u>.
Entrance fees? Yes.
Lessons? Yes and you can rent the equipment needed.
Wheelchair accessible? No.
Food? No.
Restrooms? No.

Related places of interest: Colorado History Museum; Denver Museum of Natural History; Geology Museum; Henderson Museum of Natural History; Morrison Museum of Natural History

Colorado State Capitol.
Photo: Colorado Historical Society

Native American Indians.
Photo: Colorado History Museum & Colorado Historical Society

Children's Theatre: It's fun to pretend.
Photo: Arvada Center for the Arts and Humanities

CHAPTER 5

Having More Fun: Plays, Dance, Music, Stories, and Ball Games

Making believe, pretending, imagining, creating, inventing, and entertaining...that's what you do when you want to try out being someone else, like becoming a character in a play or a movie. That's what show people and professional athletes do when they get up on a stage or in a stadium, do magic tricks, tell jokes, dance on their toes, play musical instruments, sing, or play ball. Not only is it fun to do all this yourself in your home, yard, or at a park, but it's fun to watch others do it in theaters, movie houses, auditoriums, concert halls, bookstores, parks, amphitheaters, and stadiums. You

may be surprised to find that there are so many places in this region where you can be entertained, and many of these places are described below.

PLAYS, FILMS, AND MAGIC SHOWS

Plays, films, and magic shows, all seem like magic to me. They have a way of carrying you into the story or action while you're sitting in your seat. If they are really good, you almost forget where you are and who's sitting beside you. Has this ever happened to you?

ARVADA CENTER FOR THE ARTS AND HUMANITIES CHILDREN'S THEATER

You'll get a fresh look at your favorite stories when you see them acted out on the stage. You may decide you want to read them again, and again, and again.

Where is it? At 6901 Wadsworth Boulevard in Arvada.
Phone numbers? box office, 431-3939; 431-3081, hearing impaired.
Parking? Yes, and it's free.
Other transportation? RTD buses stop nearby.
Presentations? There are two plays each season. *Charlotte's Web* and *The Three Little Pigs and Little Red Riding Hood: What Really Happened Once Upon A Time*, were shown in the 1994-95 season.
Performances on what days and hours? September through May, Tuesdays through Saturdays, 10:00 a.m., noon, or 1:00 p.m., depending on the day.
Admission fees? Weekdays, $4.00; Saturdays, $5.00. Advanced reservations required.

Children's Theatre: They're great at pretending.
Photo: Arvada Center for the Arts and Humanities

Handicap access? Wheelchair accessible; shadowed performances for hearing impaired; and special headsets for the blind and visually impaired.
Food? No.
Restrooms? Yes.
Birthday parties? Yes.

CHAUTAUQUA SUMMER FESTIVAL: SILENT AND TALKING FILMS

Have you ever been to a "silent" movie? Before they knew how to make "talking" films, you could watch a silent movie that had the story written under the pictures. And they were usually accompanied by piano music played right there in the movie house. During this film festival, you can watch silent and talking films. You'll see some films that are considered old favorites or classics, even though you'll be seeing them for the first time. Or you may see a really great film that you missed when it was at your neighborhood movie house. It's a good catch-up experience coming here.

Where is it? At Chautauqua Auditorium in Chautauqua Park, Boulder. Drive west on Baseline Road to 9th Street. The Park is on the left side of the road and the Auditorium is a short walk in the Park.
Phone number? 449-2413.
Parking? Yes, and it's <u>free</u>, in the parking lots or on the street.
Other transportation? RTD buses stop near by.
Open what days and hours? In the 1994 season, four silent films were shown on four different nights in July at 8:00 p.m. Talking films were shown in June and August at 7:30 p.m. Call for a copy of the schedule for dates and times.
Programs? The 1994 program included the following four silent films: *The Black Pirate, The Italian Straw Hat, Metropolis,* and *Safety Last.* Each film was accompanied by a live piano. Talking films, such as *Free Willy, Snow White,* and *The Many Adventures of Winnie the Pooh*, were also shown. Call for a copy of the program.
Admission fees? Children 6 years old and under, <u>free</u>; 6 to 12 years old, $1.00; adults, $2.00.
Wheelchair accessible? Yes.
Food? Yes.
Restrooms? Yes.

CHILDREN'S MUSEUM THEATER

Which will it be: a magician pulling a rabbit out of a hat, a clown walking on stilts, dancers gliding across the stage, puppets bobbing up and down, Curious George getting into trouble? Any one of these performances may be showing when you stop by the Museum. Check it out and don't miss the fun.

Where is it? At 2121 Children's Museum Drive in Denver. Take Route I-25 to Exit 211 (23rd Avenue) and go east to 7th Street. Turn right and right again on to Children's Museum Drive.

Phone number? 433-7444.

Parking? Yes, and it's <u>free</u>.

Other transportation? RTD buses, Platte Valley Trolley, and the Cultural Connection Trolley stop nearby.

Performances what days and hours? Fridays, 5:30 to 8:30 p.m.; weekends and during school holidays. Call for times.

Presentations? Shows vary but they have included magicians, puppeteers, plays, concerts, dance performances, mimes, and clowns. Call for information.

Admission fees? <u>Free</u> on Friday nights; included in the regular museum admission: members and children under 2 years old, <u>free</u>; senior adults, $1.50; 2 to 64 year-olds, $4.00.

Wheelchair accessible? Yes.

Food? Yes, in Dr. Dabble's Drive-In Cafe.

Restrooms? Yes.

Birthdays? Yes.

COLLAGE MUSEUM THEATER

See the description in Chapter 4, *Exploring Worlds,* under Collage Museum Special Exhibits, Sunday Stars, page 102. Phone, 440-9894.

DENVER CENTER THEATER COMPANY
AND PRODUCTIONS COMPANY

Plays that have been performed on stages around the world come to this theater. Sometimes, this is the first theater to perform a play and then it goes on to show in other cities. You'll see old favorites, like *A Christmas Carol*, and new ones, like *Black Elk Speaks*. The actors are usually very good and the stage settings can be very impressive. It's a treat to see a story come alive on the stage.

Where is it? At 14th Street and Curtis Avenue, at the Denver Center for the Performing Arts (DCPA), in downtown Denver.
Phone numbers? 893-4000 and 893-4100.
Parking? In the DCPA parking garage, $3.00; on-the-street, free after 6:00 p.m.; off-the-street parking lots, bring dollar bills.
Other transportation? RTD buses, Light Rail trains, and the Cultural Connection Trolley stop nearby, and it's a short walk from the Sixteenth Street Mall Shuttle.
Performances what days and hours? Call for a copy of the season's schedule.
Presentations? The Theater Company presents 12 plays each season, some of which may appeal to children. For example, in 1994-95 they presented *Black Elk Speaks, A*

Christmas Carol, and *Taming of the Shrew* which could be appealing to a wide age range. Theater Center Productions bring tours of Broadway shows. Some of the musicals, such as *Beauty and the Beast,* would be appropriate to children but are not selected especially for them.

Admission fees? The tickets range in price from $20.00 to $30.00, depending on the show, the day, and the seat. Reserve tickets in advance by calling the ticket office.

Handicap access? Wheelchair accessible; listening systems for hearing impaired; accommodations made for visually impaired when notified in advance.

Food? Yes.

Restrooms? Yes.

DENVER CIVIC THEATER

There have been a lot of great stories written in books for kids and some of these have been made into plays. Reading the story and then seeing the play (or the other way around), gives you a good idea how close the playwright is to the original story. And, you can decide which you liked best.

Where is it? At 721 Santa Fe Drive in Denver.

Phone number? 595-3800.

Parking? Off-street parking is <u>free</u>. Private parking lots are located on the north and south sides of the theater. Bring money.

Other transportation? Light Rail trains and RTD buses stop nearby.

Performances what days and hours? Saturdays and Sundays, 1:00 p.m.

Presentations? Three plays, especially for children: *Alice in Wonderland, Jungle Book,* and *Free To Be You and Me,*

169

were shown in the 1994-95 season.
Admission fees? Children, $5.00; adults, $6.00.
Wheelchair accessible? Yes.
Food? Yes.
Restrooms? Yes.
Birthday parties? Yes.

DENVER PUPPET THEATER

"Duddley the Dude says, 'For a great time, come on down to the Denver Puppet Theater.'" Why? Because as soon as you enter the door, you get a paper puppet to color. And because you get to take part in the show when the puppets talk to you. And, if that isn't awesome enough, after the show is over, you can stay and make up your own puppet shows. There are five stages and 100 puppets to choose from! Where else in the whole wide world can you do something like this?

Where is it? At 2700 South Colorado Boulevard in Denver. It is a store-front theater inside the University Hills Mall.
Phone number? 987-3612.
Parking? Yes, and it's <u>free</u>.
Other transportation? RTD buses stop nearby.
Performances what days and hours? Thursdays and Fridays, 10:00 a.m. and 1:00 p.m.; Saturdays, 11:00 a.m. and 1:00 p.m.; Sundays, 1:00 p.m. Each lasts between 35 and 40 minutes.
Presentations? Eight different plays are presented each year, such as *Beasties of the Bog*, *Three Billy Goats Gruff*, and *Stories the Animals Tell*. Many are original to the puppeteers, Annie Zuck and Mel Reum. Some are classical children's stories.

Admission fees? All over 18 months old, $3.00. Younger than 18 months-old, <u>free</u>.
Wheelchair accessible? Yes.
Food? No.
Restrooms? Yes.
Birthday parties? Yes.

DENVER VICTORIAN PLAYHOUSE

The neat thing about coming here is that you become a part of the play. The actors draw you into the story. Sometimes they'll ask what you think about what's happening on the stage, and other times they'll ask for your help. You never know what's going to happen and that's what makes coming here such fun.

Where is it? At 4201 Hooker Street in Denver. Take Route I-25 to Federal Boulevard, exit, and drive north to 42nd Street and west to Hooker. The theater is on the north-west corner.
Phone number? 433-4343.
Parking? Yes, and it's <u>free</u> on-the-street.
Other transportation? RTD buses stop nearby.
Performances what days and hours? Most Thursdays, Fridays, and Saturdays at 10:00 a.m. Call for tickets.
Presentations? There are three children's theater productions each year, and the audience is encouraged to participate. Recent productions were, *The Further Adventures of Maid Marian, Little Mary Sunshine,* and *Treasure Island.*
Admission fees: Four years old and younger, <u>free</u>; all others, $5.00.
Wheelchair accessible? No.

Food? Yes.
Restrooms? Yes.
Birthday parties? Yes.

EULIPIONS CULTURAL CENTER

This is where you can see a part of the African American cultural experience on stage. There's a special Christmas show for families called *Black Nativity*, and there are many other plays during the year that appeal to both children and adults.

Where is it? At 2715 Welton Street in Denver.
Phone number? 295-6814, information and reservations.
Parking? Yes, and it's <u>free</u>.
Other transportation? Light Rail trains stop nearby.
Performances what days and hours? Thursdays, Fridays, and Saturdays, 7:00 p.m.; occasional matinee performances on Saturdays at 3:00 p.m.
Presentations? Features approximately nine plays each year by and about African-Americans. Some of these are appropriate for children, such as *Black Nativity*, a Christmas play performed in 1994. Call for program information.
Admission fees? Ranges from $12.00 to $15.00, general admission and $8.00 to $12.00, children and senior adults.
Wheelchair accessible? Yes.
Food? No.
Restrooms? Yes.

HERITAGE SQUARE CHILDREN'S THEATER

If you like becoming a part of a play, you'll have a great time at this theater. The actor's draw you into the story, and you never know just how that is going to happen. Sometimes the plays are based on favorite stories like *The Wizard of Oz*, and at other times they are new stories. You can always depend on them to be good stories.

Where is it? At 18301 Colfax Avenue in Golden, at the inter-section of Route 40 and Sixth Avenue. Drive west on Route I-70 and take Exit 259. Drive north about one mile.
Phone number? 279-7800 Extension 13.
Parking? Yes, and it's <u>free</u>.
Other transportation? No.
Performances what days and times? Every Saturday, year-round, at 1:30 and 3:00 p.m.
Presentations? Four one-hour plays are presented each season, in repertory. *The Wizard of Oz* and *Santa's Nut Cracker* were two of the four presented in the 1994-95 sea-son. The actors call for the participation of children in the audience. Call for program information.
Admission fees? Children, $4.00; adults, $3.00.
Wheelchair accessible? Yes.
Food? No.
Restrooms? Yes.

IMAX THEATER

Do you like things that are BIG? If you said yes, you're going to love this theater. BIG is what it is! And, besides, when you see a movie here, you feel as though you were in it...no kidding! If there's a roller coaster ride on the screen, you'll feel as though you are on the roller coaster; if there's a mountain climber high up on a mountain ridge looking down at the ground, you'll feel as though you're the one up there. It's amazing, exciting, astonishing, thrilling, and out of the ordinary! It's where it's at and where you should be!

Where is it? At 2001 Colorado Boulevard in Denver, at City Park, on the 2nd floor of the Denver Museum of Natural History.

Phone numbers? members, 322-7009; nonmembers, 370-6351; hearing impaired, 470-8257.

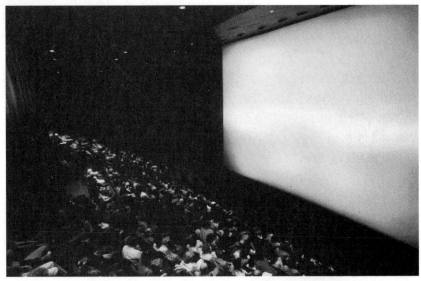

IMAX Theatre: Is this screen big or what?
Photo: Denver Museum of Natural History

Parking? Yes, and it's <u>free</u>.
Other transportation? RTD buses and the Cultural Connection Trolley stop nearby.
Open what days and hours? Everyday. Call to find out what films are showing and the times.
Programs? Films are shown on a huge, four-and-a-half story by six-and-a-half story screen, such as *Search for the Great Sharks* and *Africa: The Serengeti.*
Admission fees? Members: children, $2.25; adults, $2.75. Nonmembers: children and senior adults, $4.00; other adults, $5.00. Ask about buying a combined ticket with a planetarium show to get a better price.
Strollers? Rent for $1.00.
Wheelchairs? Yes, and they're <u>free</u>.
Wheelchair accessible? Yes.
Food? Yes.
Restrooms? Yes.

PEANUTBUTTER PLAYERS AND THE LUNCH BUNCH

If you've ever dreamt of being an actor or actress then this is a theater you'll want to see. Kids like yourself are in the plays and they are good. They've studied and rehearsed their parts so that you will think they are the person or animal they are pretending to be. Your dream of being on stage might come true if you decide to work at it, too.

Where is it? The office is at the Toadstool Playhouse at Mapleton Avenue and Folsom Street in Boulder. The November Luncheon Theater Playhouse is given at the Senior Center Theater on 9th and Arapahoe Streets; the

December Holiday Shows are given at the Penny Lane Theater at 18th Street; and the summer musical is given at Boulder High School. Call for directions.

Phone number? 786-8727.

Parking? Yes, and it's <u>free</u>.

Other transportation? RTD buses stop nearby.

Presentations? Talented children between the ages of 7 and 16 years old have performed such plays as *Cinderella, Snoopy,* and *The Electric Sunshine Man.*

What days and hours? Eight performances in November of the Luncheon Theater Playhouse on Saturdays and Sundays at noon. Two weekends in December for the Holiday Show. August performance of the big musical by the Peanutbutter Players. Call for dates and times.

Admission fees? Lunchbunch, $7.00; Holiday Shows: $3.50; Peanutbutter Players: children, $3.00; adults, $5.00.

Wheelchair accessible? Yes.

Food? Lunchbunch and Holiday Show, yes; Peanutbutter Players, no.

Restrooms? Yes.

PLAY-GROUND THEATER SUPER SATURDAYS

Do you know who Shakespeare is? If you said, yes, than you know he wrote plays a long, long time ago and many people think he's the best playwright, ever. Well, at this children's theater you can see some of his plays which were changed so that you would understand and enjoy them. They also do other plays, like *Aladdin*. This is a very original theater group. They are sure to please and surprise you. Check them out.

Where is it? At 1535 Spruce Street in Boulder, in the old Salvation Army building.
Phone number? 442-5198.
Parking? Southwest corner of 15th Street and Pine Street, in the old Salvation Army (Unity Church) parking lot.
Other transportation? RTD buses stop nearby.
Performances what days and hours? Saturdays at 2:00 p.m. and 4:00 p.m.
Presentation? In addition to adapting Shakespeare for children, such as the ones presented in the 1994 season, *Lady and the Trash (Macbeth)* and *Bottom's Tale (A Midsummer Night's Dream)*, they do such other plays as, *Fractured Fairy Tales* and *Aladdin*.
Admission fees? $4.00.
Wheelchair accessible? No, but they offer assistance.
Food? No.
Restrooms? Yes.
Birthday parties? Yes.

SOUTH PEARL STREET PRODUCTIONS

Do you like variety and surprises. Well, keep a look out for their latest plays and films. The plays are usually performed around holiday times and can be original or based on old favorites. And their movies are "oldies but goodies." There is plenty of variety and lots of surprises here.

Where is it? At the Vogue Theater, 1465 South Pearl Street in Denver.
Phone number? 722-0033.
Parking? Yes, and it's <u>free</u>.
Other transportation? RTD buses stop nearby.

Performances what days and hours? Theater: Saturday mornings and evenings; Films: Friday evenings, Saturday and Sunday mornings. Call for more specific program and schedule information and reservations.

Presentations? Original plays, seasonally, for children, such as, *Everyday Miracles,* in December and a musical, *Aladdin*, in the spring. Children's classic films are shown year-round, such as *Our Gang* and *Shirley Temple* films.

Admission fees? Children, $2.50; adults, $5.00.

Wheelchair accessible? Yes.

Food? Yes.

Restroom? Yes.

Birthdays? Yes.

THEATER IN THE PARK

Do you like to look up at the summer sky at night when it is filled with twinkling stars? Well, that's not the only place you'll see stars when you go to Theater in the Park on a clear, summer's night. You'll see a play with real actors on the stage, spinning out their own kind of magic in the stories they tell. Come early, explore this downtown Park, and eat a picnic dinner before the play begins. Then, after the play is over, look up at the star studded sky. Awesome!

Where is it? In Civic Center Park Greek Amphitheater, at 14th Avenue and Acoma Street, in downtown Denver.

Phone number? 770-2106.

Parking? On-street parking is <u>free</u>, where you find it. Off street parking lots nearby. Bring dollar bills and change.

Other transportation? RTD buses stop nearby and Light Rail trains connect with the Sixteenth Street Mall Shuttle.

Performances what days and hours? Last two weekends in July and the first weekend in August on Thursday, Friday, and Saturday nights at 8:00 p.m.

Presentations? Three family-oriented plays are presented each weekend, and one of the three is likely to be especially for children. In 1994 they presented both *The Three-Cornered Hat* and *Peter and the Wolf*. The plays are described as having broad based appeal, upbeat themes, and as being culturally diverse.

Admission fees? None. They are <u>free</u>.

Handicapped access? Wheelchair accessible, and Saturday night performances are signed for the hearing impaired.

Food? No.

Restrooms? No.

DANCE

There are so many different ways to dance and so many different kinds of music to dance to. Some music almost pulls at you and says, "Move!" It's fun to watch dancers, too, whether they're balancing up on their toes, or tapping their toes on the floor; whether they are jitter-bugging or waltzing. It seems so easy, watching them move to the rhythm of the music.

ACADEMY OF THE
BOULDER PHILHARMONIC: DANCE

Did you ever consider being a dancer...or perhaps playing the music for dancers? The dancers and the musicians in this auditorium may have felt just as you do, and here they are, dancing and playing in an orchestra. You might say that their dreams came true.

Where is it? At Mackay Auditorium on the University of Colorado campus in Boulder, and at one of the public schools in Boulder. Call for this information.

Phone number? 449-9291.

Parking? On-street metered and unmetered parking. Bring change.

Other transportation? RTD buses and the HOP shuttles stop nearby. For other concert shuttles, call for information.

Presentations? There are three multi-media concerts a year for families. In the 1994-95 season, *The Nutcracker Suite* ballet was performed four times; a birthday concert of *Carnival of the Animals* had several showings; and during the Week of the Child, *The Teddy Bear Concert* was per-formed <u>free</u>.

Admission fees? Tickets range in price, depending on where you are sitting. Call for information and reservations.

Wheelchair accessible? Yes.

Food? No.

Restrooms? Yes.

CHILDREN'S MUSEUM THEATER: DANCE

See the description earlier in this Chapter, under Plays, Films, and Magic Shows, page 167. Phone, 433-7444.

COLLAGE CHILDREN'S MUSEUM: DANCE

See description in Chapter 4, *Exploring Worlds,* under Collage Children's Museum, Special Exhibits, Sunday Stars, page 102. Phone, 440-9894.

COLORADO BALLET COMPANY

Did you know that football players study ballet techniques to develop balance and strength? Well, many of them do and you can see why they do this by watching ballet dancers perform. Wearing special shoes, they dance and twirl on their toes, not an easy thing to do, yet they make it look easy. And when they leap through the air, they come down so firmly and gracefully.

Did you ever see a story told by dancers on a stage? Not a word is spoken, yet the story is told by the way they move to the music. You can tell when they are happy or sad, unafraid or scared, eager or hesitant, calm or worried. Dance is another kind of language and ballet is a special kind of dance.

Where is it? At 14th Street and Curtis Avenue, in the Denver Center for the Performing Arts (DCPA) complex, in downtown Denver.
Phone number? 837-8888.
Parking? In the DCPA Parking Garage, $3.00. Otherwise, parking on the street, <u>free</u> after 6:00 p.m.
Other transportation? RTD buses, Light Rail Trains, and the Sixteen Street Mall Shuttle stop nearby.
Presentations? Two of the season's performances are especially well-suited to children, such as their annual

December performance of *The Nutcracker Suite*.
Performances what days and hours? Call for program, schedule, and ticket reservations.
Admission fees? $12.00 to $45.00, depending on your choice of seats.
Wheelchair accessible? Yes.
Food? Yes.
Restrooms? Yes.

MUSIC

Have you ever heard Blue-Grass, Folk, or Jazz music? What about Symphonic, Western, and Choral music? Do Barber Shop Quartets sound familiar? You can sample a whole range of vocal and instrumental music and find something that suits your taste best by attending some of the musical performance listed below.

ACADEMY OF THE BOULDER PHILHARMONIC: CONCERTS

See description above, in this chapter, under Dance, page 179. Phone, 449-9291.

CHAUTAUQUA SUMMER FESTIVAL: MUSIC

There's so much going on at this Festival that it may be hard for you to choose which musical performances are for you. Try sampling different kinds and the next time you have to make a choice, it may be easier to do.

Where is it? At Chautauqua Park Auditorium in Chautauqua Park Boulder. Drive west on Baseline Road to 9th Street. The Park is on the left side of the road.

Phone numbers? General Admission only, 440-7666; Reserved and General Admission, 449-2413.

Parking? Yes, and it's <u>free</u>, in the parking lots and on-the-street.

Other transportation? RTD buses stop nearby.

Open what days and hours? Beginning of June to beginning of September; box office opens at 7:00 p.m. for 8:00 p.m. concerts; doors open at 7:30 p.m.

Programs? There is a wide range of musical performances, including classical music of the Colorado Festival Orchestra, barber shop, blue grass, folk, and western music, and solo vocal and instrumental performances. Call to receive a copy of the program schedule.

Admission fees? General admission, $6.00 to $20.00, depending on the concert; Reserved seats, $13.00 to $25.00, depending on the concert.

Wheelchair accessible? Yes.

Food? Yes.

Restrooms? Yes.

COLLAGE CHILDREN'S MUSEUM: MUSIC

See description in Chapter 4, *Exploring Worlds,* under Collage Children's Museum, Special Exhibits, Sunday Stars, page 102. Phone, 440-9894.

COLORADO SYMPHONY ORCHESTRA

When you go to a special children's concert, you can always count on the conductor talking to you about the orchestra and the music. You'll be able to listen to the different sounds each of the instruments make. Can you tell the difference between a trumpet and a french horn, or a flute and a clarinet, or a drum and a violin? By the time you come to a few of these concerts, you'll know a lot about musical instruments and listening to music. You may even decide to learn how to play one in your school orchestra. Cool!

Where is it? At Boettcher Concert Hall, in the Denver Center for the Performing Arts (DCPA), at 14th Street and Curtis Avenue in downtown Denver.
Phone number? 986-8742.
Parking? In the DCPA parking garage, $3.00; on-the-street parking is <u>free</u> on Sundays.
Other transportation? RTD buses and Light Rail trains stop nearby and the Sixteenth Street Mall Shuttle is a short distance away.
Performances on what days and hours? There are usually three family concerts presented each season, each performed on a Sunday afternoon at 2:30 p.m. When indicated, a 4:00 p.m. concert is added. Last season, there were two concerts in October and one in December. Call 986-8742 for dates and reserved seats.
Presentations? There are two one-hour concerts for families, such as, *Beethoven Lives Upstairs* and *The Mozart Experience*, which were performed during the 1994-95 season. In addition, the Symphony presents a Halloween concert.
Admission fees? $5.00 for all, but the Halloween Concert is <u>free</u>.

Wheelchair accessible? Yes.
Food? Yes.
Restrooms? Yes.

FIDDLER'S GREEN AMPHITHEATER

If you want to see some famous musicians perform, this is where it happens. Rock and Roll, Jazz, Country Western, Folk Singers, Blue-Grass...you name it and you'll find it here. Check the season schedule when it comes out in April and plan ahead to see your most favorite, most famous entertainers.

Where is it? At 6350 Greenwood Plaza Boulevard in Greenwood Village. Take Route I-25 to the Orchard Street Exit. Turn west off the ramp and take the first left turn into the Amphitheater.
Phone number? 220-7000.
Parking? Parking costs $5.00 in the Amphitheater lots.
Other transportation? RTD buses stop nearby.
Performances what days and hours? May 1st to September 30th; evening performances. The season's schedule appears in April, in both the Denver Post and Rocky Mountain News. Call for specific information and reservations regarding appropriate concerts for children.
Presentations? Concerts by well-known entertainers.
Admission fees? General admission tickets range in price from $15.00 to $30.00, depending on the show.
Wheelchair accessible? Yes
Food? Yes.
Restrooms? Yes.

SWALLOW HILL CHILDREN'S CONCERTS

If you like music and musicians who make you smile, you'll enjoy these concerts. They are always interesting to watch and to hear because many of the concerts combine storytelling with music. Come see and hear for yourself!

Where is it? At Swallow Hill Music Hall, 1905 South Pearl Street in Denver.
Phone number? 777-1003.
Parking? Yes, and it's <u>free</u> on the street and in a small parking lot.
Other transportation? RTD buses stop nearby.
Performances what days and hours? Family programs are usually scheduled for Saturday mornings. Call for information on programs, dates, and times.
Presentations? A few concerts a year are programmed especially for families, such as *Paul Taylor and Joe Fire Crow Present Australian and Native American Stories and Music*, from the 1994 program.
Admission fees? $4.00.
Wheelchair accessible? Yes
Food? Yes.
Restrooms? Yes.

STORY READING AND STORYTELLING

While both story reading and storytelling aim to make listening to stories fun, they differ in the way each goes about doing it. Someone who reads a story, holds the book so that you can see the pictures if there are any, or so the reader can see the print. A storyteller, on the other hand, does not read from a book. He or she tells a story from memory, one which may be in a book, or one which the storyteller makes up.

Story reading and storytelling are done in several different kinds of settings, such as bookstores, theaters, libraries, shopping malls, museums, and parks. In the first three of these settings, they tend to be pre-scheduled throughout the year. In the latter three, they may occur seasonally and tend to be associated with holiday celebrations. In Kids Discover Denver and Boulder, story reading and storytelling carried out in bookstores, theaters, and libraries are listed below.

ABC BOOKS AND POSTERS: STORY READING

Do you like to listen to good stories and look at lots of good books for kids? Come over to this bookstore on Saturday mornings and you'll have a good time listening and browsing. And when you leave, you'll get a pretty sticker just for being there. That's really cool!

Where is it? At 2550 South Colorado Boulevard in Denver.
Phone number? 759-0250.
Parking? Yes, and it's free.
Other transportation? RTD buses stop nearby.
Program days and hours? Saturdays, 10:00 to 10:30 a.m.

Programs? Call for information on themes and activities.
Program fees? None. They're <u>free</u>.
Store features? Children are encouraged to browse with adult supervision. They are given a free sticker for coming in, and teachers and senior adults receive a discount on book purchases.
Wheelchair accessible? Yes.
Food? No.
Restrooms? Yes.

ARVADA CENTER FOR THE ARTS AND HUMANITIES: STORYTELLING

Do you love to have your mom or dad tell you stories about when they were kids? If you do, you should go to Storytelling at the Arvada Center, usually around holiday times. That's when they tell stories about Halloween (probably spooky ones), Christmas (probably sad-happy ones), or Easter (cute and snugly ones). And they also have storytellers visit the History Museum at the Center, where they tell stories about real people from long ago...like your grandparents...and about the pioneers and the Native Americans from in and around Arvada.

Where is it? At 6901 Wadsworth Boulevard in Arvada.
Phone numbers? Box office, 431-3939; hearing impaired, 431-3081.
Parking? Yes, and it's <u>free</u>.
Other transportation? RTD buses stop nearby.
Program days and hours? Call for information on dates and times.
Programs? In the past, the themes have related to specific

holidays and to stories about Colorado Native Americans. Call for information on current programs.
Admission fee? Call for information on cost.
Wheelchair accessible? Yes.
Food? No.
Restrooms? Yes.

BARNES AND NOBLE BOOKSTORES: STORY READING

Do you know what a "book worm" is? Do you think it's a creepy-crawly creature that lives inside books, or someone who is always reading books? If you said someone who is always reading books, you're right on the button! If you're a "book worm," you'll hear some old favorite stories and some new, hot-off-the-press stories during their special story programs at the Barnes and Noble Bookstores. After story-time is over, you can stay and look through the books on the shelves and tables, a book worm's dream.

Where are they? There are six stores at the following locations: **Denver,** at 960 South Colorado Boulevard and at 5392 South Wadsworth Boulevard; **Aurora,** at 14015 East Exposition Avenue; **Boulder,** at 1741 28th Avenue; **Greenwood Village,** at 8555 East Arapahoe Road; and **Westminster,** at 6925 West 88th Avenue.
Phone numbers? Denver: South Colorado Boulevard, 691-2998 and South Wadsworth Boulevard, 972-1468; **Aurora:** 366-8928; **Boulder:.** 444-2501; **Greenwood Village:** 796-8851; and **Westminster:** 424-2493.
Parking? Yes, and it's free.
Other transportation? RTD buses stop nearby.

Program days and hours? Denver: South Colorado Boulevard, Mondays to Saturdays, 11:00 to 11:30 a.m. and 3:00 to 3:30 p.m.; Tuesdays, 7:00 to 7:30 p.m. and South Wadsworth Boulevard, Saturdays, 11:00 to 11:30 a.m.; 3:00 to 3:30 p.m.; **Aurora:** Saturdays, 1:00 to 2:00 p.m.; **Boulder:** Saturdays, 1:00 p.m.; **Greenwood Village:** Saturdays, 9:00 to 11:00 a.m.; one Thursday a month, 7:00 to 8:00 p.m.; and **Westminster:** Saturdays, 11:30 a.m.; Tuesdays, 6:30 p.m.

Programs? Call each store for more information on themes and activities.

Program fees? None. They're free.

Store features? Children may browse through books under adult supervision. All books are discounted.

Wheelchair accessible? Yes.

BO PEEP BOOKS: STORY READING

You can tell by the name of this bookstore that children are welcome. There's a special play corner for you, too. And don't be surprised if you see a person dressed like a mouse and eating a cookie or a car dressed like a turtle. The best part, though, is when the people who wrote and drew the pictures for one of your favorite stories, tell you how they did it, and then read it to you. This place is really cool!

Where is it? At 1957 South Wadsworth Boulevard in Lakewood. Drive west on Sixth Avenue and take the Wadsworth Boulevard Exit, south. Continue to Jewell and turn into the Market Square shopping center.

Phone number? 989-8127.

Parking? Yes, and it's free.

Other transportation? RTD buses stop nearby.

Program days and hours? Throughout the year with

announcements of days and dates made in a quarterly newsletter or by phone calls made to customers requesting this information.

Programs? Story reading is primarily in conjunction with visits by book authors and illustrators, such as those from *The Magic Schoolbus* series, *If You Give A Mouse A Cookie*, and *Old Turtle*. An incentive summer reading program for elementary-aged children involves weekly awards. There is a large selection of books and a friendly, well-informed staff to serve you.

Program fees? No. They're <u>free</u>.
Wheelchair accessible? Yes.
Food? No.
Restrooms? Yes.

THE BOOKIES BOOKSTORE: STORY READING AND STORYTELLING

Can you imagine what it would be like to go to the best children's book store in Denver? If you're a "Curious George" kind-of-person, you'll want to come to Bookies and experience the real thing. You're likely to get caught up in a "Charlotte's Web" of cuddly creatures, some of whom you'll recognize as being from your favorite story books. And, if you get as hungry as a "Mother Goose's" gosling, there are pretzels to snack on. But don't forget the special story and activity times. They're a real treat.

Where is it? At 4315 East Mississippi Avenue in Denver.
Phone number? 759-1117.
Parking? Yes, and it's <u>free</u>.
Other transportation? RTD buses stop nearby.

Program days and hours? Saturday mornings, year-round.
Programs? Call for information about themes, activities, and author-signings.
Program fees? None. They're <u>free</u>.
Store features? It provides an inviting and stimulating atmosphere for kids of all ages. There are lots of cuddly toys to snuggle up to and books, books everywhere to browse through. There are pretzels to snack on, too. This bookstore received the designation of "Best Children's Bookstore" two years running in *The Best of Westword* annual awards. All books are discounted. It's also one of the few stores, nationally, that is able to put your child in a video adventure.
Wheelchair accessible? Yes.
Food? Yes.
Restrooms? Yes.

BOULDER BOOKSTORE: STORY READING

You may know the story of *The Three Little Pigs,* but what about *The Three Little Wolves and the Big Bad Pig,* or *The True Story of the Three Little Pigs,* or *The Three Pigs and the Fox?*

At the Boulder Bookstore, you may hear these other piggy stories at their Story Reading time, as well as other great stories, like *Alexander and the Terrible, Horrible, No Good, Very Bad Day,* or *Sylvester and the Magic Pebble,* or *Where the Wild Things Are.* Afterwards, you can tell the stories back to yourself while you look through the books.

Where is it? At 1105 Pearl Street in Boulder.
Phone number? 447-2074.
Parking? <u>Free</u> in city parking lots with a validated bookstore

ticket, or with tokens for metered on-the-street parking.
Other transportation? RTD buses stop nearby.
Program days and hours? Call for dates and times.
Programs? Call for information on themes and activities.
Program fees? None; it's <u>free</u>.
Wheelchair accessible? Yes.
Food? Yes.
Restrooms? Yes.

CHAUTAUQUA PARK AUDITORIUM: STORYTELLING

Storytelling becomes a great stage performance at Chautauqua Park Auditorium. It's one kind of special experience to be up close to the storyteller and another kind of special experience to be part of a large audience, seeing and listening to gifted storytellers. Which special experience do you prefer?

Where is it? Drive west on Baseline Road to 9th Street in Boulder. The Park is on the left side of the street. The Auditorium is a short walk into the Park.
Phone number? 449-2413.
Parking? Yes, and it's <u>free</u> in parking lots or in the neighborhood.
Other transportation? RTD buses stop nearby.
Program days and hours? Call for information on times and tickets.
Programs? During the Chautauqua Summer Festival (see description above under Music), the 1994 program presented storytelling as part of a multimedia event, *Living A Dream*. They also scheduled two performances of *Storytellers Are Us*.

193

Program fees? Call for information.
Wheelchair accessible? Yes.
Food? Yes.
Restrooms? Yes.

COLLAGE CHILDREN'S MUSEUM: STORYTELLING

At this Museum, they have special people who are so good at telling stories to children that you want them to go on and on and on, telling more and more stories. After you hear these storytellers, you'll know the difference between having a story read to you from a book, and having a story told to you from memory. The next thing to do after hearing a great storyteller, is to become a storyteller yourself, and retell the story to a friend.

Where is it? At 2065 30th Street between Pearl and Walnut Streets in Boulder.
Phone number? 440-9894.
Parking? Yes, and it's <u>free</u>.
Other transportation? RTD buses stop nearby.
Program days and hours? On the first Sunday of every month. Call for times.
Programs? Stories are told by a member of the Colorado Storyteller's Guild. Call for information on themes.
Admission fees? Call for information.
Wheelchair accessible? Yes.
Food? No.
Restrooms? Yes.

THE HUE-MAN EXPERIENCE BOOKSTORE: STORY READING AND STORYTELLING

Have you heard the following stories: *Amazing Grace, Tar Beach, Snowy Day, My First Kwansaa Book, Happy Birthday, Martin Luther King*, and *Whistle for Willie*? If you have, you might want to hear them again because they're so good. In addition, the main characters are Black people. The Hue-Man Experience bookstore is where it's at when it comes to great story books like these. You can always count on hearing stories read or told about African Americans when you come here at their special story times each month. And you'll always think of it as being a truly human experience!

Where is it? At 911 Park Avenue West in Denver.
Phone number? 293-2665.
Parking? Yes, and it's <u>free</u>, on-the-street.
Other transportation? RTD buses stop nearby.
Program days and hours? The third Saturday of every month, between 1:00 and 2:30 p.m., stories are read or told which are of interest to children up to ten years old.
Programs? Call for information on themes and activities.
Program fees? None. They're <u>free</u>.
Store features? Specializes in Afro-American adult and children's books and is reputed to sell the largest volume of these books, nationally.
Wheelchair accessible? No.
Food? No.
Restrooms? Yes.

195

PUBLIC CENTRAL LIBRARIES:
STORY READING AND STORYTELLING

Are you and your library good friends? If not, you're sure to be once you start going to library story times. The librarians at the library know how to make stories come alive, especially old favorites. Discovering new stories is fun, too. Between story times at your library, you can borrow picture and story books, take them home, and bring them back to the library when you're ready for some more good stories to hear and to borrow all over again.

Where are they? In your community; look up the address of the library nearest you or phone the central library to get this information.
Phone numbers? Central Libraries: **Denver**, 640-8800; **Arapahoe County**, 220-7704; **Arvada**, 424-5527; **Aurora**, 340-2290; **Boulder**, 441-3099; **Englewood**, 762-2550; **Evergreen**, 674-3389; **Golden**, 279-4585; **Lakewood**, 232-9507; **Littleton**, 795-3961; **Westminster**, 430-2400.
Parking? Yes, and it's free. Check on availability when you call.
Open what days and hours? Ask about this when you call.
Programs? Both the Central and Branch Libraries are likely to have story reading or storytelling programs for preschool and school-aged children. Some have additional activities involving crafts and books. In the summer, they may have a motivational reading program for children; if a child reaches a goal, she or he earns a prize. They are planned from season to season, some only for as long as special funds are available. Call your community library for information.
Program fees? None. They are free.
Wheelchair accessible? Yes.

Food? No.
Restrooms? Yes.

THE TATTERED COVER: STORY READING

When you go to the Tattered Cover, you'll be at one of the best known bookstores in the U.S.A. It was among the first to create a comfy bookstore for "book browsers" of all ages. You'll find the children's books on the lower level, with various alcoves, where you can search for picture and story books to tickle your fancy before and after story reading times.

Where are they?: There are two Denver stores at the following locations: **North Cherry Creek Shopping Area,** at 2955 East First Avenue; and in **LoDo,** at 1628 16th Street.
Phone numbers? Cherry Creek: 322-7727; and **LoDo:** 436-1070.
Parking? Cherry Creek: Yes, and it's free with a store-validated ticket; and **LoDo,** at 16th Street and Wynkoop Avenue.
Other transportation? RTD buses stop nearby.
Program days and hours? North Cherry Creek: Tuesdays, 11:00 to 11:45 a.m.; Saturdays, 10:30 to 11:15 a.m.; **LoDo:** at the time of this writing, a schedule had not been determined. Call for information.
Program fees? None. They're free.
Store features? It has gained a national reputation for its relaxed atmosphere, extensive inventory, and helpful salespeople. Books are discounted to teachers.
Wheelchair accessible? Yes.
Food? Cherry Creek: Yes; **LoDo:** Yes.
Restrooms? Yes.

WALDENKIDS BOOKSTORE: STORY READING

Do you know how you can travel to places you've never visited before, or play games you never played before, without moving from where you're sitting? If you said, "By listening to stories," you guessed right! Stories can take you anywhere. You could go with a small hippopotamus in *Harry at the Airport*, or with Lena and Lila, the Leaping Lizards, in *Circus*, or with a bunch of curious woodland creatures in *Elmer Blunt's Open House*. Waldenkids will help you to travel like this when you come to their story times. Try not to miss them.

Where is it? At the Crossroads Shopping Mall in Boulder.
Phone number? 440-0271.
Parking? Yes, and it's <u>free</u>.
Other transportation? RTD buses and/or HOP shuttles stop nearby.
Program days and hours? Tuesdays, 11:00 a.m. and Thursdays, 3:00 p.m.
Wheelchair accessible? Yes.
Food? No.
Restrooms? Yes.

WATCHING THE PROFESSIONALS PLAY BALL GAMES

Most kids like to play catch and run and tumble after a ball, just for the fun of it. And there are so many different ways to play ball. You can catch it, hit it, kick it, punch it, and throw it into a basket. Playing ball in the park is one kind of game. Watching the college pros and the real professionals play in a stadium, surrounded by cheering and booing crowds, is another kind of ball game altogether. It's great entertainment and something families can enjoy together.

COLORADO FOXES SOCCER TEAM

If you think soccer is great fun to play or to watch, you're bound to enjoy seeing the Colorado Foxes play at Mile High Stadium. You might get some good ideas to try out at your own game. Careful you don't get "horse" or get a "frog in your throat" from cheering too long and too loud for your team.

Where is it? This American Professional Soccer League (APSL), plays at Mile High Stadium, at 2755 West 17th Street in North Denver.
Phone number? 840-1111.
Parking? In parking lots around the stadium. Bring money.
Other transportation? RTD buses and the Platte Valley Trolley stop nearby.
Open what days and hours? The season begins in May and ends in September. Games are played on different days of the week and start at 7:00 p.m. There are approximately 15 home games played each season. Call for information on dates.
Admission fees? $5.00, $7.00, and $10.00, depending on where the seats are located.
Wheelchair accessible? Yes.
Food? Yes.
Restrooms? Yes.

COLORADO ROCKIES BASEBALL TEAM

"Take me out to the ball game..." is the first line of a song that was popular many years ago. It reminded me that baseball has been a favorite spectator sport for a long, long time. Don't you love to see the pitcher wind up to get ready to pitch the ball? Have you figured out why the catcher wears a metal fence over his face? Isn't it fun to see the batter slide into base? See how the crowd leaps out of their seats when he hits a home run. Which position do you think you'd like to play?

Where is it? This Denver-based, National Baseball League (NBL) team, play at Coors Field, at 20th and Blake Streets, in lower-downtown Denver.
Phone number? 292-0200, for information and tickets.
Parking? At the time of this writing, the Field had not been completed and parking policies had not been established. Call for information.
Other transportation? Call for information.
Open what days and hours? At the time of this writing, a schedule had not been finalized. The Field is expected to have an opening-day celebration in April. Call for information.
Admission fees? Call for information.
Wheelchair accessible? Yes.
Food? Yes.
Restrooms? Yes.

Related places of interest: Colorado Fireworks Softball Tourney (July)

DENVER BRONCOS FOOTBALL TEAM

WOW! Watching the Denver Broncos play football is awesome! Each of the players is so big and brawny and powerful. It's easy to see why they wear special helmets, teeth protectors, and padding for their shoulders and knees. Look! There goes Elway! If it wasn't for the big number on his back, I wouldn't have known. Even though the players run fast, they still get knocked, whacked, bumped and bruised. I guess that's why football is called a contact sport.

Where is it? This Denver-based National Football League (NFL) team, play at Mile High Stadium, at 2755 West 17th Street in north Denver.

Phone numbers? 433-7466, tickets and schedules; 649-9000, other information.

Parking? In parking lots around the stadium. Bring money.

Other transportation? RTD buses and the Platte Valley Trolley stop nearby.

Play what days? Pre-season games, late summer; season runs from September through December, with approximately 8 home-games. Call for days and times.

Admission fees? Varies, depending on location of seats and type of tickets; season tickets and single event tickets sold. Call for prices.

Wheelchair accessible? Yes.

Food? Yes.

Restrooms? Yes.

DENVER NUGGETS BASKETBALL TEAM

You gotta jump, dribble, slam-dunk, pass, and shoot! Keep moving! Watch Mutombo! Those Denver Nuggets know how to keep their eyes on the ball and move fast. Watch that scoreboard! Those numbers are climbing high!

Where is it? This Denver-based National Basketball Association (NBA) team plays at McNichols Sports Arena at 1635 Clay Street in Denver.
Phone number? 893-3865, for information and tickets.
Parking? In city and private parking lots around the stadium. Bring money.
Other transportation? Platte Valley Trolley, RTD buses, and Light Rail trains stop nearby. Bring exact fare for buses.
Play what days? Early November to late April, 42 home games are played. Call for dates, times, and tickets.
Admission fees? Varies, depending on the game and location of the seats. Call for ticket prices.
Wheelchair accessible? Yes.
Food? Yes.
Restrooms? Yes.

UNIVERSITY OF COLORADO
BUFFALOS FOOTBALL TEAM

You can see why they call the team, The Buffalos. They all look as determined and powerful as their namesakes, and they have a strong, winning record. Do you know which is the quarter-back, half-back, and full-back? Can you spot the wide-end and tight-end receivers? Have you seen the offensive and defensive line-men? Where's the head coach and how many assistants does he have? What do all those arm movement mean? If you haven't figured out who's who and what's what in the game, you can always enjoy the cheer leaders and join them in cheering your team on. Many of the players you're seeing today, are going to be playing for national league teams tomorrow!

Where is it? This football team plays at Folsom Field, off Folsom Avenue between Colorado and Arapahoe Avenues, in Boulder.

Phone numbers? 492-8377, ticket and schedules; 492-5331, other information.

Parking? In public lots around town, including the Euclid Avenue parking structure which has a shuttle to Folsom Field.

Other transportation? RTD buses stop nearby.

Play what days? Approximately six home games each year, on Saturdays, through the fall months. Call for dates and times.

Entrance fees? Varies, depending on location of seats and type of ticket; season tickets and single event tickets sold. Call for tickets prices.

Wheelchair accessible? Yes.

Food? Yes.

Restrooms? Yes.

UNIVERSITY OF COLORADO BUFFALOS WOMEN'S BASKETBALL TEAM AND MEN'S BASKETBALL TEAM

Here are two more teams of which Coloradans are proud. They've made their marks, man-to-man and woman-to-woman, on the court. Many of your senses get a workout here. You can see a lot of action as the players rush back and forth across the court. You can hear the ball pound the floor when it bounces or dribbles before it becomes airborne, headed towards the basketball net. You can smell the sweat of the players as they point and shoot. You can taste the saltiness of the chips and the coolness of the pop. Don't miss the Women's and Men's Teams in action. They'll make your skin tingle every time they score.

Where are they? These two basketball teams play at Coors Events Center on Regent Drive, between Broadway and Colorado Avenue, in Boulder.

Phone numbers? 492-8337, tickets and schedules; 492-6877, other information on men's games; 492-6086, other information on women's games.

Parking? Yes, and it's <u>free</u>, at a parking structure or in parking lots by Coors Event Center.

Other transportation? RTD buses stop nearby.

Play what days? There are 17 games played by the men's team and 16 played by the women's team in Boulder each year. Call for days and times.

Admission fees? Varies by location of seat and type of ticket; season tickets and single event tickets sold. Call for ticket prices.

Wheelchair accessible? Yes.

Food? Yes.

Restrooms? Yes.

Cider Press at work.
Photo: Lakewood's Historical Belmar Village

CHAPTER 6

Looking Ahead:
Adventures by the Month

There are many fairs, festivals, and special events that recur each year because of the success they have experienced with the public in previous years. In the pages that follow, those of particular interest to children and their families are listed, alphabetically, by the month in which they occur. Browse through the months' activities so that you can choose which will suit your family best.

A Visit with Santa.
Photo: Four Mile Historic Park & Kris Nicovich

January

Bald Eagle Day: A two-week celebration of the return of the wintering bald eagles to the Rocky Mountain Arsenal National Wildlife Refuge. It includes viewing live bald eagles, wildlife tours, exhibits, educational programs and a special Family Day. Call 289-0232 for dates and times.

Colorado Indian Market and Western Art Roundup: This is a four-day market and celebration of Indian art from North and South America. You will see paintings, beadwork, pottery, jewelry, sculpture, baskets, and weavings. Native American food, music, dance performances, and fashion shows abound at Currigan Exhibition Hall in downtown Denver. It's held in July also. Call 447-9967 for more information.

Martin Luther King, Jr., Birthday March: A parade in downtown Denver to honor the famous civil rights leader. Call 640-2678 for information.

National Western Stock Show and Rodeo: At the Denver Coliseum, 4655 Humboldt Street (Route I-70 and Humboldt Street), for two weeks in January, 9:00 a.m. to 9:00 p.m. Admission is charged. It has been called the world's largest cattle show and among the largest rodeo shows. It includes horse shows, horse and cattle auctions, sheep shearing contests, many educational displays, a junior animal show and sale, Children's Ranchland, buffalo, goats, llamas, miniature and draft horses, and specialty acts. Don't miss the **Stock Show Parade** through downtown Denver prior to the opening and after the show is over. Call 297-1166 for information.

February

Buffalo Bill's Birthday Celebration: February 26th at the Buffalo Bill Memorial Museum, Route 5 off I-70, Golden. Call 526-0744 for information.

Collage Children's Museum Birthday Celebration: Art workshops and musical performances help celebrate this occasion at this Boulder Museum the first Sunday in February. Call 440-9894 for information.

Denver Auto Show: Held at the Colorado Convention Center in downtown Denver. This is a huge display of new cars and pick-up trucks. Children are welcomed and may go inside the cars and trucks if supervised by an adult. Call 831-1691 for dates, times, and cost of admission.

March

Boulder Bach Festival, Kids for Bach: There are two days of events, one in March and the other in April. Both are held at the Boulder Main Library and are <u>free</u>. Early in March, on a Sunday, there are two afternoon performances of Bach's music by children who auditioned and were selected to play at this concert, using a variety of instruments. Call 494-3159 for dates and times.

Channel 4 Education EXPO: This five-day fair encompasses all of the Colorado Convention Center in downtown Denver. It features hands-on activities for all ages in every area of learning. In the past the learning pavilions included exploring science facts behind science fiction, doing science experiments, participating in mini-art classes, designing and constructing with Tinkertoys, testing out properties of water and other sources of energy, learning about the body's organs, and taking an up-close look at sheep, cattle, and other farm animals. Plans call for inclusion of the Cub Scouts, Boy Scouts, and Eagle Scouts Adventure Show, where outdoor sports are demonstrated. Students pay $2.50; adults, $3.50. Starts the end of March and runs into April. Call 988-3803 for more information.

Kids Fair: Held at Currigan Exhibition Hall, downtown Denver. Companies that deal in products and services for children, exhibit them here. There is a great deal of entertainment that would appeal to children ranging from puppet and magic shows to story reading and storytelling. (No phone number given; call the Convention Center, 640-8000).

March Pow-Wow: at the Denver Coliseum at 4655 Humboldt Street (Route I-70 and Humboldt Street). It is the largest gathering of Native American, West and Midwest Indians. There are drum and dance-group competitions and reenactments of the brave deeds of past battles. Call 455-4575 for information.

St. Patrick's Day Parade: This is the nation's second largest St. Patrick's Day parade and it's held in downtown Denver. Call 399-9226 for information.

Shrine Three-ring Circus: At the Denver Coliseum, 4655 Humboldt Street (Route I-70 and Humboldt Street), from the end of March through early April. Shows include elephants, lions, tigers, bears, clowns, trapeze artists, and wire-walkers. During intermission, bicycles are given away to anyone holding a program with a particular signature in it. Times vary by day. General admission in advance, $6.00; at the door, $7.00; reserved, $10.00. Call 455-8172 for days, times, and tickets.

Tri-State Auto Show: This is for specialty cars, only, such as antiques, classics, street rods, and race cars. It's for looking,

Early car.

Photo: Colorado Historical Society

not touching. Children under 5 years old, <u>free</u>; 6 to 12 year-olds, $2.00; adults, $8.00. Call 457-4810 for dates.

April

Boulder Bach Festival - for Kids: Late in April, on a Sunday afternoon, the Boulder Bach Festival Orchestra and Chorus present a concert for children at the Boulder Main Public Library. Call 457-4810 for the date and time.
Celebration of 1860s Work and Play: At the Four-Mile Historic Park in Denver, it features old time baseball and farming, along with stagecoach or hay rides, in this

living-history setting. The farmers and crafts people wear costumes of the 1860s and demonstrate their work skills. Admission for children under six years old, <u>free</u>; 6 to 15 year-olds and senior adults over 65, $3.00; other adults, $5.00. Call 399-1859 for dates.

Channel 4 Education EXPO: See the description under *March*, above.

Earthfest: Celebrated in Larimer Square, downtown Denver. It features over 70 environmental organizations, booths, entertainment, and workshops for kids. Call 534-2367 for information.

Earthday Celebration at the Collage Children's Museum: Children learn about recycling in interesting and powerful ways at this Boulder museum. Call 440-9894 for date and time.

Earth Day Celebration at the Denver Museum of Natural History: Preserving our resources, animal, mineral, and vegetable, is the theme. Call 322-7009 for information and reservations.

Easter Egg Decorating and Hunt: It's happening at the Natural History Museum in City Park, Denver, and it's fun. Call 322-7009 for information and reservations.

Easter Egg-stravaganza: It's on schedule at the Denver Children's Museum. Call 433-7444 for date and time.

Kinetic Conveyance Parade: Held the last Saturday in April at 1:00 p.m., around the business loop in downtown Boulder, one week prior to the Kinetic Conveyance Parade. All participants in the Race show off their costumes and floats, and perform goofy skits in front of the Boulder Theater. Call 694-6300 for information.

Shrine Three-ring Circus: Presented at the Denver Coliseum, 4655 Humboldt Street (Route I-70 and Humboldt Street) from end of March through early April. (There is also a Shrine Circus in July.) Shows include elephants, lions, tigers, bears, clowns, trapeze artists, and wire-walkers. During intermission, bicycles are given away to anyone holding a program with a particular signature in it. Show times vary by day. General admission in advance, $6.00; at the door, $7.00; reserved, $10.00. Call 455-8172 for days, times, and tickets.

May

Boulder Creek Festival: This award winning festival is held at Central Park, along a section of Boulder Creek, over a 2½ day weekend. A parade starts it off and is followed by dancing to "oldies but goodies" music, and two days of over 25 fun-filled events. These include a rubber duckie float competition and race, storytelling, dancing, singing, listening to bands, looking at endangered animals, craft exhibits, a juried art show, the Children's Kingdom, and much, much more for all family members. Call 441-3400 for more information.

Cinco de Mayo Celebration: Denver celebrates its Hispanic heritage on Santa Fe Drive. Call 534-8342 for information.

Furry Scurry, Denver Dumb Friends League Benefit: Bring your pets to Washington Park and take a two-mile walk in the Pet Parade or in the Kids Derby. You can pre-register or register on the day of the event and make your pledge. Call 791-6166 for information.

213

Kinetic Conveyance Race: This race is held the first weekend of May at Boulder Reservoir, all day. The kinetic conveyances are vehicles that have been engineered to drive on land, and through mud and water. Each pulls a float that is creatively designed and crafted and is theme-related. There's lots to see, such as a volley ball tournament and Hot Air Balloons. A per-car entry fee is charged. Call 694-6300 for information.

Kops 'N Kids: A bicycle race begins and ends in City Park at East High School in Denver, for kids from 6 to 16 years old and Denver's police officers. After the race, food is available, and there are lots of games, activities, and demonstrations of the work of the police with young people. Call 863-1633 for information.

Memorial Day Parade: This event is in recognition of United States soldiers who gave their lives in battle during wars and military operations. The parade is held in downtown Denver. Call 640-2678 for information.

June

Busker Rendezvous: Street performers, professional and amateur, do their stuff over the first full weekend in June, starting Friday evening. There's entertainment for all the family, with jugglers, musicians, magicians, sword swallowers, and more! It is held at the Downtown Mall in Boulder. Call 449-3774 for dates and times.

Cherry Blossom (Sakura) Festival: Held outdoors and indoors at Sakura Square and in the Community Center next to the Buddhist Temple, in downtown Denver. It's a weekend of Japanese folk dances, fencing, art, poetry, music, and food. Call 295-1844 for information.

Colorado Renaissance Festival: This outdoor theme fair recreates medieval 16th century England with knights, crafts, jugglers, jesters, food, and more. It is held in Larkspur, near Castle Rock, for eight weekends, from early June to the end of July. Call 688-6010 for information.

Conservation Day at the Denver Zoo: During the day, there is a lively combination of performances and hands-on activities, such as live animal demonstrations, games, entertainment, and turning trash into treasures with recycled items. At 7:00 p.m., a special presentation is given, followed by a tour of an exhibit. Call 331-5808 for information.

Denver International BuskerFest: Held on the main thoroughfares of downtown Denver, to provide two-days of entertainment by jugglers, clowns, magicians, and other talented performers. In keeping with Busker tradition, after each performance, the hat is passed for the audience to show their appreciation. Call 534-6161 for dates and times.

Japanese Festival: A cultural event, held at the Denver Botanic Gardens. Call 777-7372 for information.

Juneteenth Celebration: This is a four-day celebration commemorating Black pride and the end of slavery. It is held in the Five Points area of Denver. There is gospel and choir singing, street dancing, a parade, a beauty pageant, an essay contest, and kiddie rides. To add to the festive air, vendors sell food, clothes, and crafts. Call 399-7138 for information.

MAGIC Street Dance: Held at Larimer Square in downtown Denver. The street is closed to traffic and open for dancing. Call 534-2367 for information.

National Trail Days: Children and adults are invited to participate in restoring the land at the Rocky Mountain Arsenal National Wildlife Refuge by collecting and planting native grasses and wild flower seeds, and by learning about the importance of protecting the land and the wildlife on the Refuge. Call 289-0232 for activities, dates, and times.

People's Fair: Begun originally as a neighborhood pride fair in Capitol Hill, this fair got so big that now it is held at Civic Center Park in downtown Denver. There is music, crafts, and food booths, dancing, and other entertainment. Call 830-1651 for information.

Rocky Mountain River Festival: This family-oriented, four-day fair occurs the third weekend in June on the campus of Arapahoe Community College in Littleton. It's objective is to raise money for a humanitarian cause. There are concerts, food, arts and crafts booths, carnival rides, and a pavilion devoted to children's hands-on activities. Nearby, raft rides and races are held on the Platte River. Call 794-2131 for information.

Springspree Festival: Held at the Denver Center for the Performing Arts at 14th and Curtis. This is a weekend of <u>free</u> outdoor performances of music and mime, and a special children's program as well. Call 893-4000 for information.

July

Buffalo Bill Days: A three-day celebration held in Golden at Lions and Parfet Parks and other city sites, as well as at the Buffalo Bill Museum on Lookout Mountain. In Golden, there are activities for all family members: a talent show; a parade; a children's fair with rides, games, face-painting, and crafts activities; square dancing; an ice-cream social; and more. This is a fund raiser for the city of Golden, so fees are charged for some activities. On the third day, at the Museum, the staff dress in costumes of the 1800s, a Buffalo Bill look-alike rides around on a horse, there's a barbecue and

The Big Show.
Photo: Buffalo Bill Memorial Museum

other events, and a graveside ceremony, all of which is <u>free</u>. Call 279-3113 and 526-0744 dates and times.

Colorado Fireworks Softball Tourney: At the Broomfield Community Center, the top girls' softball teams in the country, 12 years old and younger, compete over a three-day period. Call 420-0203 for dates and times.

Colorado Indian Market and Western Art Roundup: This is a four-day market and celebration of Indian art from North and South America. You will see paintings, beadwork, pottery, jewelry, sculpture, baskets, and weavings. Native American food, music, dance performances, and fashion shows abound at Currigan Exhibition Hall in downtown Denver. Held in January also. Call 447-9967 for more information.

Denver Black Arts Festival: A two-day celebration of the visual and performing arts produced by Black artists is held at City Park. A Children's Pavilion involves children in a wide-variety of art activities related to different cultures from which Black people come, including various countries in Africa and South America. There is music, theater, dance, storytelling, and drama performed on five stages; exhibits from the Denver Museum of Natural History, Black American West History Museum and Heritage Center, Denver Zoo, and Denver Botanic Gardens; work done by over 50 recognized visual artists; food from local restaurants; and more. Call 293-2559 for information.

Fourth of July Fireworks in Boulder: A fireworks display starts after the sun sets at Folsom Stadium in Boulder. Come early and join in on the sing-along. Call 442-1044 for information.

Old-fashioned Fourth of July Family Picnic: At Four-Mile Historic Park in Denver, this celebration features stagecoach or hay wagon rides, and costumed farmers and craft people, such as blacksmiths, quilters, bee-keepers, and gold-panners. Admission for children under six years old, <u>free</u>; 6 to 15 year-olds and senior adults over 65, $3.00; other adults, $5.00. Call 399-1859 for dates.

August

Adams County Fair and Rodeo: Held in Commerce City the first or second week of August, from Wednesday to Sunday, from 10:00 a.m. until the last event closes. Although there is a $2.00 per car fee to the fair grounds, there are many <u>free</u> events for families to attend, such as the Livestock Show, the Four-H Show, and the Children's Pavilion. In addition, there is <u>free</u> entertainment throughout the day. There is a per ride fee at the Carnival, and entry fees to the Rodeo and Truck-and Tractor-Pull events. Call 659-3666 for dates, directions, and admission fees.

Chile Harvest Festival: Held at the Denver Botanic Gardens in collaboration with the Chicano Arts and Humanities Council, this is a celebration of Spanish colonial folk art of southern Colorado and northern New Mexico. Traditional foods are served and there are singers, dancers, and mariachi performers throughout the day. Call 370-8187 for date and tickets.

Passport to Asia Festival: The many different ethnic groups from Asia are celebrated at this festival held in Currigan Hall the first weekend in August and sponsored by the Asian Pacific Development Center. There are booths showing the crafts of each group, cultural awareness programs, marshall arts demonstrations, and special Asian arts and crafts activities in the Children's Corner...something for all family members. Call 355-0710 for information.

Two Free Days at the Denver Museum of Miniatures, Dolls, Toys: Take advantage of this opportunity to get acquainted with this Museum. Call 322-3704 for dates.

219

September

Colorado Performing Arts Festival: A two-day, outdoor, free celebration of the performing arts held at the PLEX (Denver Performing Arts Complex), downtown Denver, over the last weekend in September. Ballet, opera, cowboy poetry, storytelling, gospel singing, reggae music, and country western music are performed by talented Colorado artists. There are lots of hands-on activities for kids, such as creating "junk" and wire sculptures and making flags and banners. Call 640-2678 for information.

Fiesta! Fiesta!: A two-day, outdoor, neighborhood celebration of Mexico's independence from Spanish rule on upper Larimer Street. Music, dancing, food, and fun for all the family. Call 322-2300 for information.

Free Day at the Denver Museum of Natural History: A great opportunity to visit this fabulous museum. Call 370-6351 for information.

Labor Day Parade: A march through downtown Denver in recognition and celebration of the role of working people in our society. Call 640-2678 for information.

Organic Fair: At Four-Mile Historic Park, there are two days set aside for celebrating the harvesting of the organically grown vegetables from their big garden. In addition, there are stage coach or hay wagon rides, and demonstrations by the costumed farmers, blacksmith, quilters, cloth-makers, lace makers, and others. Admission for children under six years old, free; 6 to 15 year-olds and senior adults over 65, $3.00; other adults, $5.00. Call 399-1859 for dates.

Rocky Mountain Air Fair: The aim of this six-day fair is to promote aviation in the Rocky Mountain region. It has been at Currigan Exhibition Hall in past years but may locate at Wings Over the Rockies Aviation and Space Museum next year. A large space is devoted to a children's educational area, Fantasy of Flight, which consists of 12 hands-on learning stations. There is one on weather, another on down-drafts, aircraft instruments, what makes a plane fly, and so on. Children receive a Log Book as they enter the first station, and before moving on to succeeding stations, they are signed out. They keep the Log Book as a memento. Call 367-0670 for more information on location and dates.

October

African Arts Family Day: Held at the Denver Art Museum in downtown Denver, from 12:00 to 5:00 p.m. Call 640-2793 for information.

Boo at the Zoo: The Denver Zoo presents this pre-Halloween fun day from 10:00 a.m. to 4:00 p.m. Children may wear their costumes. There are trick and treat doors, a haunted maze, clowns, jugglers, and face painters. Call 331-4100 for information.

Cider Days: Belmar Museum and Historic Village in Lakewood, celebrates fall the first weekend in October. There are exhibits of antique autos, crafts, and other antiques, and lots of entertainment, including face painting, clowns, and mimes. Food and drink are sold. Call 987-7850 for information.

El Dia De Los Muertes: This Latino holiday is celebrated at the Collage Children's Museum along with Halloween. Call 440-9894 for date and time.

Free Day at the Denver Museum of Natural History: A fabulous opportunity for Colorado residents to go to this outstanding museum free of charge. Call 370-6351 for the date.

Halloween Concert: Fun at the free Sunday 2:30 performance and parade with the Colorado Symphony Orchestra at Boettcher Concert Hall. Call 986-8742 for information.

221

Kids Halloween Parade: Costumed kids assemble on the Courthouse lawn in Boulder at 1:00 p.m., October 30th, for singing and stories. Then, all parade through the downtown mall. Call 449-3774 for information.

One Sky, One World International Kite Fly: Held on one Saturday in October at Cramner Park, 3rd Avenue and Clermont Street, in Denver. Call 433-9518 for date and time.

Pumpkin Festival: This celebration of the season is held at the Chatfield Arboretum the second Saturday in October. It is a fun-filled family festival, where you'll be able to buy your pumpkins, gourds, Indian corn, and corn stalks...all grown here; enjoy the craft activities; buy good food from vendors; and take hay rides. Call 973-3705 for information on times and entrance fees.

Ringling Brothers and Barnum and Bailey Circus: There are acrobats, tightrope walkers, animal acts, and clown shows at the Denver Coliseum for about ten days. Watch the train unload and see the **Elephant's Parade** to the Denver Coliseum at 4655 Humboldt Street (Route I-70 and Humboldt Street). Call 296-7469 for dates, times, and ticket prices.

Rocky Mountain Book Festival: There are many, many activities for children of all ages at this four-day festival celebration of books held at Currigan Exhibition Hall. It's free. Call 447-9967 for dates and times.

Run for the Zoo: This is a fund-raiser for the Denver Zoo, with pledge-packs for children and adults. Registration is required. Call 331-4100 for information.

Spirits of the Past: A Halloween event at the Four-Mile Historical Park, 6:00 to 9:30 p.m. There are re-enactments of historical scenes from the old days and storytelling. Cider is served free. Admission for children under six years old, free; 6 to 15 year-olds and senior adults over 65, $3.00; other adults, $5.00. Call 399-1859 for dates.

Trick or Treat Street: A Halloween celebration at the Denver Children's Museum. Call 433-7444 for dates and times.

November

Rocky Mountain Pet EXPO: Live pets of all kinds, from the familiar to the unfamiliar, are on display for all to see. You'll see reptiles, birds, pot bellied pigs, ferrets, cats, and dogs of many breeds. And there are lots of events scheduled for children by KID Radio, Channel 2, and others. Call 696-6100 for more information.

Turkey Trot at Washington Park: This 5K event includes children as well as adults, making it a festive Thanksgiving family event. Call 640-2678 for information.

Veterans Day Parade: Held in downtown Denver in recognition of all United States veterans who fought in all the wars. Call 640-2678 for information.

December

Blossoms of Light: A holiday celebration held at the Denver Botanic Gardens on York Street. A path of lights is lit in the outdoor and indoor gardens which is to be followed. Various activities are planned. Call 370-8187 for information on activities, days, times, and tickets.

Christmas at Fiske Planetarium: A holiday planetarium celebration to collect food for the homeless at the Planetarium in Boulder. Storytelling by members of the

Rocky Mountain Storyteller's Guild. Call 492-5002 for date and time.

Christmas Tree Cut: Areas of forests are designated for cutting your own tree. There is a limit set in any particular area, so submit your application early along with your $10.00 fee. A four-wheel drive vehicle is recommended. Call 275-5755 for information.

First Night Colorado: The last night and first day of the year is celebrated in downtown Denver on December 31st. Activities start at noon, geared mainly for families. Evening events, mainly for adults, continue until midnight. Call 399-9005 for information.

Holiday Open House at Four-Mile Historic Park: Two days in December, you can see a Christmas celebration from the 1860s to 1880s at this Denver site. Children can frost and eat home-baked cookies, see an old-fashioned St. Nicholas, take a stage-coach ride and sleigh rides if there's snow, and make their own tree-ornaments. There's story-telling as well. Admission for children under 6, free; 6 to 15 and senior adults, $3.00; other adults, $5.00. Call 399-1859 for dates and times.

Kwansaa Celebration: This seven-day African celebration of the harvest is held at the Collage Children's Museum in Boulder. Call 440-9894 for dates and times.

Lights of December Parade: Carolers in costume, colorful floats, and bright lights are part of this festive holiday parade in downtown Boulder. Call 449-3774 for information.

Mayor's Tree Lighting: Held at the Belmar Museum and Historic Village in Lakewood the first Friday in December. The community's Christmas Tree is lit by its Mayor; there is singing; doughnuts and hot cocoa are served. Call 987-7850 for information.

Noon-year's Eve: At the Denver Children's Museum, December 31st, from noon to closing. Call 433-7444 for information.

Parade of Lights: This holiday parade draws the largest crowds to downtown Denver all year. It is a very festive event. Call 640-2678 for information.

Wildlights at the Denver Zoo: Held every evening during the last three weeks of December, from 6:00 to 9:00 p.m. There are activities for all family members. The zoo grounds are lit up, there is storytelling, carollers, and other live entertainment. Hot cider and roasted chestnuts are served. Call 331-5808 for information.

TOWN INDEX

Brighton

Broomfield

Commerce City

Englewood

GENERAL INDEX

C

I

M

N

National Center for Atmospheric Research [497-1174 *and* 497-1173]:   129
  Nature Preserve [441-3950]:   75
  Nature Trails [441-3950]:   50
National Earthquake Center [238-1500]:   131
National Trail Days [289-0232]:   215
National Western Stock Show and Rodeo [297-1166]:   208
National Western Stock Show Parade [297-1166]:   208
Native American Indian Culture: 104,110,117,124, 141,208,210,218
Nature Center, Lookout Mountain [526-0594]:   49,73
Noon-year's Eve [433-7444]:   225

O

Organic Fair [399-1859]:   220
Old Fashioned Family Fourth of July Picnic [399-1859]:   218
One Sky, One World International Kite Fly [433-9518]:   222
Ornithologists, Denver Field [279-3076]:   66,72

P, Q

Parade of Lights [640-2678]:   225
Parades: 208,210,212,214,215,220,222-225
Passport to Asia Festival [355-0710]:   219
Peanutbutter Players [786-8727]:   175
People's Fair [830-1651]:   216
Pioneer Museum, D.A.R. [279-3331]:   108
Planetarium, Charles C. Gates [322-7009 *and* 370-6351]:   95
Planetarium, Fiske [492-5002]:   120
Platte River Greenway [698-4011]:   38
Platte Valley Trolley [458-6255]:   17
Playgrounds: 21-53
Play-Ground Theater Super Saturdays [442-5198]:   176

USEFUL TELEPHONE NUMBERS

Boulder Mountain Parks System: 441-3408
Boulder Parks and Recreation: 441-3400 and 441-3950
Boulder Visitor's Bureau: 442-2911
Colorado Convention Center: 640-8000
Colorado State Parks: 866-3437
Coors Events Center: 492-8337, tickets and game schedules
Coors Field: 825-0401
Cultural Connection Trolley: 299-6000
Currigan Exhibition Hall: 640-5106
Denver Coliseum: 295-4444, information and tickets
Denver Mountain Parks: 697-4545
Denver Parks and Recreation: 964-2580
Denver Visitor's Bureau: 892-1505
Folsom Field: 492-8377, tickets and schedules
HOP Shuttle: 447-8282
Libraries:
    Arapahoe County: 220-7704
    Arvada: 424-5527
    Aurora: 340-2290
    Boulder: 441-3099
    Denver: 640-8800
    Englewood: 762-2550
    Evergreen: 674-3389
    Golden: 384-8000
    Lakewood: 232-9507
    Littleton: 795-3961
    Westminster: 430-2400
Light Rail Transit (LRT), also known as Metropolitan Area
Connection (MAC): 299-6000
McNichols Sports Arena: 893-3865, tickets; 640-7333, events

Metropolitan Area Connection (MAC), also known as Light
  Rail Transit (LRT): 299-6000
Mile Hile Stadium: 458-4849
Parks and Recreation
  Aurora: 695-7200
  Denver: 866-3437
  Englewood: 762-2575
  Evergreen: 674-0532
  Golden: 279-3331
  Lakewood: 987-7800
  Littleton: 798-2493
Platte Valley Trolley: 458-6255
Regional Transportation District (RTD): *Denver*, 299-6000;
  Boulder, 443-0100
Sixteenth Street Mall shuttle: 299-6000

NOTES:

NOTES:

NOTES:

Additional copies of this book may be ordered from the Publisher at $12.95 each plus $2.00 shipping for the first book and $.75 for each additional book per order. Add sales tax if applicable. Denver residents add state and city tax (7.3%); other Colorado residents pay state tax only (3.0%) and RTD tax, if applicable (0.8%). Please make checks payable to:

Discovery Press Publications

and mail to:

DISCOVERY PRESS PUBLICATIONS
P.O. BOX 201502,
DENVER, CO 80220-7502